THE KILI SUMMIT CLUB

THE KILI SUMMIT CLUB

One Family's Climb to the Roof of Africa

VERN JONES

WITH JILL AND RYAN BIGBY, JULIE AND JUSTIN HURLEY, AND IRENE JONES

PRINCIPIA
MEDIA

The Kili Summit Club: One Family's Climb to the Roof of Africa
© 2017 Vern Jones

Published in the United States by Principia Media, LLC

Principia Media, LLC
678 Front Avenue NW
Suite 256
Grand Rapids, MI 49504
www.principiamedia.com

ISBN 978-1-61485-308-4

Photo Credits:
Unless otherwise noted, all photos are from the personal library of Vern Jones and Family.

Cover and Interior Design: Frank Gutbrod
Cover Photograph by Samson Saitoti
Digital Imaging: Sherry Baribeau sherrydirk productions

22 21 20 19 18 17   7 6 5 4 3 2 1

Printed in the United States of America

TABLE OF CONTENTS

INTRODUCTION
The Kili Summit Club

We greatly admire the dedicated porters and guides of Mt. Kilimanjaro who make the climb possible. With their continual guidance, our climb, and my dream, became a reality.

The day before our climb, our lead guide, Philimon, meticulously inspected our gear to make certain we were properly equipped to make our trip a success. His attention to detail, along with suggestions about packing and what to leave behind, allowed us to rest peacefully the night before the climb. Our second guide, Sunday, joined us on the way to the trailhead gate. We were immediately impressed with his grasp of the English language, his knowledge of the mountain, and his understanding of the various cultures. Our third guide, Emmanuel, met us at the Machame Gate. His easy-going personality immediately fit in with our group. During our climb, we were impressed with how they guided us through the maze of trails toward Uhuru, while giving medical advice and first aid when needed. Along the way, they taught us the rich history of Mt. Kilimanjaro and about the people who live and work around the mountain. We learned about one another's families and enjoyed many of their Swahili phrases and songs.

Like many climbers, we had a few disagreements and misunderstandings at times during the climb. Some are described in this book. However, as our communication and understanding of their perspective improved, our confidence in their guidance grew. By the time we were ready to take on the final summit push, we had complete faith in their advice. We knew that barring any serious illness or tragedy, these three young men would help us fulfill our dream of standing triumphant at the top of Uhuru.

As we found out more about each guide, we learned that becoming a guide was a significant undertaking. Many guides first serve several years as porters, while working hard to gain the experience necessary to become trained as certified guides.

Even after they complete the required guide certification program offered by Kilimanjaro National Park, it is still a long shot to gaining a position with a prominent guide company. Because there is a surplus of guides and few positions available, the guides are in a poor bargaining position. Abuse of the guides is common, with many guide companies paying well below the suggested pay scale, as recommended by the Kilimanjaro Guides Association (kilimanjaroguidesassociation.org). According to KGA, the best guide companies pay $30 to 60 per day for the lead guide and $20 to 40 for each assistant guide. Some guide companies are reported to pay as little as $10 per day to the guide or even no salary, instead expecting the climbers to compensate guides with tips at the end of the journey. Though tipping is encouraged by most guide companies, in an effort to make the climb more affordable they commonly recommend a tip far below the recommended rate (as was done by our guide company).

Our first exposure to the porters occurred as we were observing the total chaos at the entrance gate at Machame trailhead. Outside the gate, hundreds of young men line up, hoping to be selected as porters by a guide. How strange it must be to awaken every morning, pack the provisions you might need in your meager backpack, and make the trek to the gate not knowing if you would be returning home in a few hours or be gone for a week.

Inside the gate, the hundreds of lucky young men who had been selected were rushing around to pack the large backpacks of the climbers, tents, sleeping bags, and all of the food and drinks that would last for the entire seven days, all the while making sure that individual backpacks didn't exceed the maximum weight of 20kg. In the chaos we met one of our porters, Kennedy, who, in addition to his basic duties as a porter, would also be the primary waiter for our climb. Kennedy joined us in the pavilion and presented us with our first meal on the mountain—a wonderful lunch, complete with a checkered tablecloth.

As each day passed and each climb became steeper, we marveled at how speedily those young men ascended, while carrying much more weight than us. While we were outfitted in appropriate layers of clothing and meticulously fitted boots, incredibly many of the porters wore canvas tennis shoes and cotton shirts. With the severe inclines and little footing, the porters passed by us with precision as they headed to ready our next camp. Then, the moment we left each morning, they began breaking camp and once again passed us so they could welcome our arrival with a hot dinner. We were surprised by how many of them spoke English (or were learning several languages), in hopes of someday becoming a guide.

In their rush to get to camp well in advance of the climbers, the porters often take risks that result in falls and injuries. During our climb, we witnessed a couple of falls; one nearly resulted in a serious injury to Jill, as well as the porter. These falls are a daily occurrence, and many of these young men become injured for life.

As with the guides, the supply of available porters is very high. This often results in terribly cruel treatment in a variety of ways. Thankfully, the Kilimanjaro Porters Assistance Project (kiliporters.org) is attempting to address this problem by setting standards regarding the pay and the treatment of porters.

KPAP recommends a maximum load for each porter of 25kg (55 lbs.). Unfortunately, these recommendations are often exceeded. The recommended porter wage is $10 per day, with an anticipated tip of $10 per day. As you might guess, many pay far less than the recommended salary, and many guides fail to distribute the tips fairly to the porters. The most recent survey indicates that nearly 30 percent of non-KPAP guide companies provide fewer than two meals per day.

Prior to our climb, we read about the abuses of the guides and the porters and made a point of asking each of our guides if he had ever experienced mistreatment. All three confirmed that earlier in their careers, they had witnessed the situations reported by KPAP.

While we climbed the mountain, the images of these poor, hardworking, ill-equipped men haunted us. Though we planned to tip generously, we felt we needed to do more.

During our ride across Tanzania, on our way to our post-climb decompression and safari in the Ngorongoro Crater, we were disappointed at the lack of gear and souvenirs proclaiming that we had successfully made it to the roof of Africa. It was then that we realized we had to find a way to do something more for those who had risked so much to make my dream come true. Later that evening, while I got a well-deserved massage, the idea of the Kili Summit Club began to develop. At dinner that evening, we discussed the idea, and everyone embraced it whole-heartedly.

Once home, working with designers in West Michigan and Seattle, we created some unique "Bragging Gear" to allow climbers to proclaim that they are members of an exclusive club of people who have followed their dream to the top of the "Island in the Sky," Mt. Kilimanjaro. You are invited to check out our beautiful apparel, glassware, patches, window stickers, and other items at Kili Summit Club (*kilisummitclub.com*).

We work with the non profit Kilimanjaro Guides Association (KGA), and all profits from the sale of our Bragging Gear go directly to the porters to help provide climbing gear and funds for medical expenses from injuries occurring on the mountain. In addition, you can also choose to reward your guide by indicating his name and KGA number in the space provided on the order form. This will allow your guide to receive a commission on each order you place.

While at the site, you can join the international online registry of climbers and share your accomplishment.

We hope you enjoy our story and look forward to seeing your name in the registry.

Chapter 1
THE ISLAND IN THE SKY

VERN

Setting my alarm wasn't necessary. I was wide awake well before it would have had a chance to ring and in plenty of time for our meeting with Philemon. The night before, I had packed all three of my bags—a small duffle with clothes and equipment for our post-climb safari; a large backpack containing everything, including two changes of clothes, for our ascent to the summit; and a small auxiliary backpack with three liters of water and snacks for use on the first day of the climb.

After a shower, my last for seven days, I knocked on the door of my daughter Jill and her husband, Ryan. They were waking up to the song "Africa."

As sure as Kilimanjaro rises like Olympus above the Serengeti…

Nice touch.

On our way to breakfast, we were joined by Julie and Justin. Soon, our conversation took on a hushed tone—something that seldom happens in our normally talkative group—as we made last-minute changes to

The Machame starting gate

the plan for the climb, while defending our food from marauding monkeys. After many months of planning and training, it was "the day" we had been waiting for.

At this point, we had spent two days in Tanzania, all the while trying to see Mt. Kilimanjaro in the distance, but to no avail. The sky on the horizon had been continually cloudy. That was too bad, since on most sunny days one can see Uhuru Peak from up to six hours away. After breakfast, as promised, Philemon arrived ready to load the Land Rover for the three-hour trip. We had met him briefly the day before, while getting acclimated to the altitude during a walking safari. Afterward, he meticulously inspected our gear to make sure it was ready for the climb. While very helpful, he was clearly a man of few words and, from what we could tell, seemingly no personality. Our talkative group might be a challenge for him. Once packed in the vehicle, we were ready to begin our trip to Machame Gate, the trailhead on Kili.

JILL

That first morning I remember lying awake, staring into the mosquito netting and waiting to start the day. Ryan's phone woke us up with the oh-so-familiar tune, Toto's "Africa." We hugged and kissed one another good morning in anticipation of an experience we had trained for over the past six months. I jumped in the shower and prepared to soak in the last remaining minutes of cleanliness, which I knew I wouldn't feel again over the next seven days. My clothes were packaged in several Ziploc bags and wrapped again in a garbage bag to protect them from getting wet from possible rain. Being a chronic over-packer, and not the tidiest of people when it comes to my bedroom, I amazed myself by packing so little—plus, it was well organized.

We headed off to breakfast to enjoy the hotel amenities for the last time before Philemon arrived to take us away from running water, beds, mosquito netting, electricity, and the everyday comforts we normally take for granted.

RYAN

I was excited about finally seeing the glistening peak of Mt. Kilimanjaro (also known as Uhuru Peak). Being from Seattle, we're used to seeing Mt. Rainer during clear days, which at 14,409 feet is pretty impressive. Mt. Kilimanjaro, however, stands at 19,341 feet. That is roughly the height of Rainer, plus a mile of straight vertical. While it was comprehensible on paper, the reality of being in its shadow, ready to climb, made me appreciate why fewer than half of the people who attempt to summit actually make it to the top. What did my father-in-law get us into?

The night before, Philemon, our head guide, came to the Mt. Meru Game Lodge to introduce himself and make sure we had the proper equipment to make the climb. We stayed at the lodge two nights to get acclimated to the altitude, catch up on sleep, and enjoy amenities, including the shower.

My backpack was filled to the rim with around a dozen extra-large Ziploc baggies filled with various clothing articles suitable for multiple climate zones. In turn, the baggies were packed into a larger-size black garbage bag, which was then stuffed into my main backpack. This, I felt, would ensure nothing would get wet. A couple of my friends had climbed Mt. Kilimanjaro, and their advice was to wrap everything in garbage bags to keep our gear dry.

Only things left to check were my team flags: Seattle Seahawks 12th Man and Washington Huskies (Go, Dawgs). Got 'em! Okay, time to get the show on the road.

JUSTIN

I had trouble sleeping and remember waking up at 2:00, 4:00, 4:15, 4:37, 5:22, and 6:43. All I could think about was the incredible journey we had in front of us and how we got to this point—all the shopping, planning, training, and so on. The morning of the trip finally dawned, and I asked my wife, Julie, "Are you up?"

Kili partially obscured by changing cloud cover

Sign posted on a tree at Mt. Meru Game Lodge

Even though we had packed our bags the night before, we somehow forgot to pack a "leave-behind" bag at Mt. Meru Game Lodge. No problem, we improvised by turning a heavy-duty garbage bag wrapped with masking tape into something adequate to hold our extra gear.

IRENE

On the first day of the climb, my morning at the home front started pretty early with a call from Julie and Justin for their kids, Bodin and Reese. They had arrived at their base camp, but they had a three-hour delay and were hoping to finish that day's portion of the climb before nightfall. The kids were excited to hear Julie's voice and her stories about how the monkeys stole food from people. Their giggles were contagious. It was a great way to start the day.

Justin and our guide Emmanuel

Later in the day, Vern called to let me know about their first day of the climb. He called me from Machame Camp, altitude of 9,842 feet. Amazingly, they had phone service! He said it was brutal and straight up and that everyone had made it, though they were all exhausted. He also told me that Julie's knee had given out halfway through the climb. That surprised me. Julie never had issues with her knees before. I thought Vern would have struggled with that a bit, since he had his knees replaced, but didn't mention my concerns because I did not want to put any negative thoughts into his head. To me, the climb couldn't end soon enough.

Although we stayed busy all day, I really didn't enjoy our time apart. When we finally arrived home, there was a surprise awaiting. Vern had ordered flowers before he left and had them delivered during their climb. Also included were gift packages for both Bodin and Reese. Vern had thought of everything before he left.

VERN

As Philemon wound the Land Rover through the small villages, we noticed the locals were busy buying, selling, and trading in the marketplace. The Maasai, in their bright red and orange attire, herded various livestock, including cows, goats, donkeys, and chickens, throughout the village.

The ride became infinitely louder and more interesting after we picked up our second guide, Sunday—an outgoing man who spoke English very well and had a wealth of knowledge (which he would share with us over the next seven days). He immediately began learning our names and relationship to one another, while giving a brief history of how he became a guide.

Safari vehicles

On our way to Arusha National Park

Mid-sentence, he pointed over Justin's shoulder and said, "There. Right there. Do you see Uhuru?" We all jumped to the left side of the Land Rover and strained our eyes to catch a glimpse of the summit, but nothing was visible.

"I don't see anything."

"Me neither."

"I've got nothing!"

Sunday simply smiled. "No, look up!"

I raised my sights above the horizon, where I was accustomed to seeing the mountains in Colorado or even Mt. Rainier in Washington State. There, in the middle of the clouds, was a faint outline of the glaciers that surround Uhuru!

They call Mt. Kilimanjaro "the Island in the Sky," which is an apt description. Looking way up, we could see the magnificent mountaintop framed by the clouds on the horizon, seemingly floating higher than any land any of us could have imagined.

Holy shit! Hello, Kili.

Over the years, I'd seen countless photos and videos of the mountain, but nothing prepared me for that moment. Following a series of exclamations and profanities, a silence fell until Jill broke it: "Dad, what did you get us into?"

The challenge now lay bare in front of us; however, I knew we were all ready. Every one of us had put in the time and the training and procured the right gear. Most important, we were mentally prepared for the climb through a competitive spirit we all shared. Each of us fully understood the challenge at hand.

JULIE

Though Kili, according to Google Maps, was only a forty-five-minute drive, we were told it would take three hours to get there. We could not figure out why until we made a couple of stops for clean water and at a tourist trap of sorts—something I didn't mind. We purchased bracelets that read, *"Pole, Pole,"* which means "slowly, slowly" in Swahili. Little did we know how much of a mantra that would become over the next week.

Back on the road, viewing Kili for the first time, we finally witnessed the majestic peak, visible through a gap in the clouds. Our entire

A diverse group gathers to climb Kili

Maasai people performing a traditional dance

group reacted audibly with gasps, laughs, very wide eyes, and remarks of astonishment. We knew the mountain was tall, but seeing it in person—literally halfway up into the sky, from our perspective—was an incredible moment. That's when the trip became real for me.

JUSTIN

Just after leaving the lodge, we learned Philemon and our other guides had decided to stop for breakfast, while we visited a small store to pick up bottled water and spare batteries. Then, on the way back to the truck, locals selling bracelets lettered with typical phrases used on the Mt. Kilimanjaro climb surrounded us. I'm not someone who buys tourist stuff, so I declined and continued my walk back to the truck. However, the rest of our group found the bracelets interesting and decided to stop. Next thing I knew, Julie and I had spent twenty bucks on trinkets.

Once back in the truck, everyone compared bracelets, while we continued waiting for the guides. Finally, after what seemed like a long breakfast, they reappeared, asking if we'd found everything. I thought to myself, *Yeah, I found everything. Let's get going.* We sure didn't expect to be waiting so long for them to return. Now we understood why it was a three-hour trip.

Continuing on our trip, we soon picked up our second head guide. I remember him jumping into the truck and immediately greeting us with a hello and wishing us a great day. His name was Sunday, and everyone seemed to completely understand what he was saying— except for me. Instead, I asked him to repeat his name, which he explained by naming the days of the week, "It's like, Thursday, Friday, Saturday, SUNDAY." That made everyone in the family a little embarrassed for me. It was the same when I met Philemon and butchered his name. That was until someone in his group called him Philly, and I went with it.

As we proceeded on our drive, suddenly Sunday interrupted his own conversation to point out Uhuru. To see it, I had to kink my neck upward. I remember saying, "Are you kidding me? That's our destination?" Goose bumps, chills, excitement, you name it—those were the emotions and physical reactions that came pouring out after I viewed that incredible sight. All descriptions pale, even after seeing numerous pictures and videos of the mountain. I was blown away.

JILL

It was a cloudy day. As we drove through Arusha, we kept our eyes on the horizon, looking for the mountain all of us had studied and

Informational signs at starting gate

Emmanuel, Vern, Jill, and Julie just minutes into our climb

Ryan checking out the plant life

dreamed about. Our new guide Sunday interrupted the silence with the announcment that he was able to see his beloved Kili! We all looked and looked for the peak, but no one could see it until Sunday instructed us to look up. As soon as the words left his mouth, I heard Justin yell, "Oh, shit!" I was on the other side of the truck and quickly crowded to his side, so I could see the tallest freestanding mountain in the world. Justin had to point it out, because I was not looking high enough. You would think, being from Washington State, I would know how to spot a huge volcano, but where I come from, they stand 14,000 feet, not 19,000 feet—and the difference is enormous. Oh, my god! "Dad, what have you gotten us into?"

We eventually took a left off the main highway to start a steady incline up to the gate, signifying the beginning of our ascent. Once we were there, it became abundantly clear we were not the only people who thought climbing that volcano was a good idea. There were vehicles everywhere, filled with people ready to attempt summiting Mt. Kilimanjaro.

VERN

At the Machame Gate we encountered total chaos. As soon as our truck wedged into a small parking spot, we all piled out, ready to stretch our legs and begin the climb. But instead, we found ourselves completely surrounded by backpacks, bags of fruit, vegetables, water bottles, and people—hundreds of people, all milling around. Philemon directed us to follow Sunday to a small gazebo, which was filled with groups of climbers awaiting instructions.

For the climb, we were required to hire an appropriate number of guides and porters, based on the total weight of the food and the equipment

Chaos at the Machame Gate

Jill, Ryan, Vern, and Justin eating our gourmet lunch

carried. Initially, that number was twelve porters and two guides for our group of five. Of course, I wasn't told that number was a wild guess, and the final number would be determined just prior to the climb. I soon realized that if there was a system to the process, it certainly wasn't apparent.

We were in a parking lot about the size of a football field, with food being thrown from one person to another. Our backpacks were gone, and our truck had been moved to allow more trucks to enter. Soon, we were introduced to our third guide, Emmanuel, who told us they were bargaining with the authorities about how many additional porters and guides were required. It was time to relax and wait, something I'm not good at in the best of circumstances, a trait passed along to the rest of the family. Besides, it was the last thing I wanted right then. After all, we were there to climb a mountain.

While waiting, we were served lunch by our waiter, Kennedy—a very tall, thin man with a big smile who spoke fairly good English. He politely invited us to move over to a recently vacated table, where he spread out a red-checkered tablecloth. He then uncovered our lunch, which consisted of hot soup and fresh bread. We noticed the groups around us were eating sack lunches. Amid the confusion, at least we were dining in style.

Unfortunately, as we dined, we watched the other groups, including those that arrived after us, begin their ascent. Still, we waited for our seemingly passive guide to lead us on our journey. With each passing moment, we questioned whether we had hired the right group for the climb.

Prior to the trip, I had done extensive research and talked with several people—including our wonderful tour guide, Eileen, who

More chaos at Machame Gate

had hired the same lead guide for her own climb eighteen months earlier. However, the day before we arrived, we learned that the guide originally hired for our climb had become sick, so Philemon had been elevated to lead guide.

Pacing around the gazebo, I decided to take advantage of the clean toilet facilities one last time. There I was greeted by a toilet I'd never experienced. It was made of the familiar porcelain; however, it was simply a bowl mounted flat to the floor with a ridged area for two feet and a far-too-small opening between the two. Due to the precise aiming requirement, there was also a mop supplied for those who lacked the required accuracy. Hopefully, my aim would improve during the trip.

That first day we were surprised by the number of climbers and the differences in the various types of climbing gear and equipment. As Sunday explained, some of the climbers who had departed earlier actually planned on spending only one or two nights on the mountain and would not attempt to summit.

JUSTIN

Once we'd reached Machame Gate, it was hard to find a spot to unload our gear. I noticed that Philly looked back at Sunday and nodded. Sunday then instructed us to grab our daypacks and pointed us toward the shelter. At that point I was absolutely jacked and ready to start the climb. Instead, we sat in the shelter, waiting.

Ryan at the Machame Route starting point

Eventually, we were introduced to Kennedy, the porter responsible for water, food, and just about anything else we were to consume. Nice guy, very friendly, and, at about six feet, six inches tall, easy to spot. Kennedy announced it was lunchtime. Unlike other groups, who had boxed lunches, we were treated more formally with a bowl of warm celery soup served on a red-checkered tablecloth. It was damn good. But, unfortunately, in the meantime most of the other climbers had begun the journey through the rainforest and up the mountain. The disappointment of being the last group to start was discouraging.

JULIE

It was pure chaos at Machame Gate. There were crowded clusters of porters scattered about the parking lot. All sorts of transport vehicles carrying groups of climbers were creatively and dangerously parked

Vern and Sunday with our destination in the background

into whatever wedge of space they could find. Added to that were tons and tons of equipment and food laid out helter-skelter, contributing to the chaos. In this beehive of activity, equipment and provisions were being loaded, one at a time, into the giant totes the porters used to carry about fifty pounds' worth of stuff, both ours and theirs.

It was a United Nations of climbers, who could be heard speaking several different languages. Jill and I had a good laugh when we caught a gentleman from Japan, right in the middle of the crowded space, doing an interesting form of Tai Chi that included some rapid pelvic thrusts.

We were so ready to go, but, as we watched group after group depart, we wondered what could possibly be taking so long. An hour passed, then another, and then a couple more. Our impatience was put on pause, however, when it was time for lunch. We all felt pretty special when a porter named Kennedy brought us our food on actual plates with real silverware atop a red tablecloth. The meal of celery soup and bread was very good. Before the trip, I had worried about the food being awful, but I was extremely impressed.

JILL

Parking our van at the Machame Gate required us to squeeze into what seemed like the last spot left to safely park a vehicle. Our backpacks were unloaded, and we were assigned our own personal porter, who was going to be carrying our stuff. We would have the same porter during the entire trip. My porter was a tall, lanky man with a kind smile, named Kennedy, who spoke broken English. He also did double duty as our waiter.

More information signs

Monkey in Tanzania

Jill heading up the trail on Day 1

Justin on Day 1

Kingfisher

There was much hustle and bustle, with porters packing food, water, and camping supplies. Most of them had waterproof bags filled to the brim with even more objects tied to them. Each was standing in line, waiting to have his bags weighed to make sure he did not carry more than the maximum weight allowed. It is recommended that each porter carry no more than 20kg (44 lbs.), plus his own gear. We were told to wait under the packed pavilion filled with other climbers, where we placed our backpacks on the only remaining bench space.

Soon, we were fighting to keep our stuff straight from other climbers', who were not shy, nor did they care, about maintaining their personal boundaries. We waited and waited. At first, the pavilion was pretty entertaining, as we walked around taking pictures and reading the "points to remember" board carved in wood, warning of the dangers

Ryan and Vern signing in

Vern and Jill signing in

and precautions of being at such altitudes. There was a huge group from Japan, who huddled around a single outlet, powering up their electronics. In the meantime, we continued to wait and wait.

As the pavilion became less crowded, a table opened up, allowing us to sit. After three hours passed, Sunday came by to say we were still waiting to sign in but that it could happen at any time. Because it was time to eat, our guides set up a colorful traditional plaid printed tablecloth and lunch, featuring an outstanding hot soup, sandwiches, and hard-boiled eggs. Everyone else, we noticed, was eating cold sandwiches wrapped in cellophane.

While waiting, we passed time by watching the blue monkeys bicker and play. One European family had their lunch stolen from them the moment they were distracted in conversation. Those mischievous little animals even unzipped the backpack of one trusting hiker, who had left it there for the looting. Thank god for the monkeys and their entertainment, or I swear I wouldn't have made it through such an excruciating wait.

At one point, my dad slipped away to check in back home with Irene, in case he wouldn't be able to get through to her again on the mountain. I could not make out what he was saying, but his tone, facial expression, and body language looked like a little kid at Christmas who was about to sit on Santa's lap.

The route we were taking up Kili was called Machame, also known as the Whiskey Route—a fitting name, since I had brought along a mini airplane bottle of Jack Daniels for the summit (not a good idea, by the way). I don't remember what time we arrived that morning, but

Justin and Julie waiting to sign in

I do recall the chills running down my back as we started to unload the vehicle. And ... it was a complete cluster fuck. So many people. Hundreds of porters running around and gathering supplies, an international stew of teams jockeying to sign in, guides figuring out how many porters they needed (our team of five required twenty-one porters and three guides). It was a little overwhelming. At this point, Philemon told us to wait under a crowded shelter, where we would meet our third and final guide, Emmanuel.

With Emmanuel, we immediately felt welcome. Like one of his own. He was extremely polite (as were all the guides), a little smaller in physique compared to the others, but charismatic and full of energy. He let us know they were in the process of tying up loose ends, getting our climbing permits, making sure the porters were accounted for and that we had enough supplies. Okay, sounded like a good plan to me. Then an hour went by, then two, and finally three. We were hungry and getting a little grumpy.

VERN

Finally, it was our turn. Philemon had us sign some paperwork, and we were off.

The first couple of hours were easy. We started on a groomed trail the width of a two-track country road. But from the pictures we'd seen from past climbers, we knew things would become more challenging. Gradually, the trail narrowed, as the inclines steepened through the heavily forested landscape. I was surprised at the lack of animals and the rather sparse bird population. With the warm sun shining, most of us wore shorts and short-sleeved base layers.

Just as the sun began setting, we caught our first glimpse of the camp, which was populated by tents grouped by the colors of the various climbing companies. Oddly, there were no fires anywhere, in spite of falling temperatures. We wore gloves, layers, and stocking hats at dinner. As would be the ritual every night, we were served a hot meal with tea, while sharing tales of the day's climb, followed by a briefing of the next day's itinerary by one of the guides.

When dinner was over, I learned about Julie's knee. It was swollen and very sore. How in the world had she injured it on our first climb? Though the trail was steep in places, she hadn't suffered any kind of fall or obvious stress. It was very strange for someone in Julie's top physical condition.

Luckily, we were well prepared for dealing with her injury. In fact, Jill had just competed classes on applying Kinesio tape at her physical therapy group. I also had experience myself, having had multiple knee surgeries, the last two being total knee replacements. During the next few days, Jill applied the magical tape, and I offered advice on navigating climbs with knee pain.

My Fitbit indicated that I had climbed the equivalent of 127 flights of stairs during our five-hour climb and challenged me to try to reach 150. I had a feeling we'd meet that challenge soon.

JULIE

The first part of the route was a firmly packed two-track dirt road that followed a slight incline. Machame Camp was 9,350 feet in elevation or seven miles away and, per our guides, approximately five to seven hours, climb. We set out at what seemed a reasonable pace, led by a third guide named Emmanuel, whom we had met just hours before departure. However, within forty-five minutes, my right knee began giving me problems, and it turned into searing pain after an hour and a half. What was going on? This was not yet a climb or even much of a hike. I decided to ignore it, hoping it would go away.

Our guides encouraged us to consume at least three liters of water per day, which is exactly what our Camelback bladders held. Because my personal bladder is the size of a grape, I knew finding a private place to urinate would be a frequent issue for me. Thankfully, on our first day's climb, there were wooden buildings sheltering toilets spaced frequently along the path. Unfortunately, the toilets consisted of a hole in the ground with two raised wooden planks on either side for your

Plant life on Kili

feet. They were horrific, and many times, because of the overpowering smell, we instead opted to go behind a bush.

JILL

Soon after starting our climb, my dad and I stopped to get our picture taken. We had the brightest, most excited looks on our faces. It was as if the last few hours had melted away, and we had our eyes on the prize.

On the service road where the climb started, we were asked to keep up a steady pace, in order to reach camp while there was still daylight. During this, the rainforest portion of the hike, the trail consisted of packed-down mud, with fallen and cut trees lining the outside. As we walked through the lush green forest, the trail was at an incline. I couldn't believe how green the forest was, with moss dripping from every tree branch, native begonias, and ferns as big as cherry trees. Emmanuel explained the plant life along the way. It was becoming clear our guides were well versed about their beloved Kili, the plant life, and the history of the land. There were also carved wooden signs marking all of the indigenous plants along the way. Some plant life looked similar to what we see in the Pacific Northwest, though they looked exotic and new framed by the African landscape.

Although we were surrounded by trees, I could tell the sun was getting closer to setting. Optimistically, it looked like the tree line marking the camp was close by. Sure enough, when we emerged from the trees, just prior to dusk, there it was. We had made it to the first camp. As we walked through the camp, there were clusters of tents everywhere. I imagined it was what a Civil War camp must have looked like. Also

Maasai village

suggestive of stepping back in time was the total lack of modern luxuries. We heard languages from all over the world, along with the sounds of clanking pots and pans and plenty of laughter. Before we were able to drop our bags, we all had to sign in and register. For me, Day 1 was a success.

Our camping arrangements consisted of a tent for each couple, plus one for my dad. Luckily, the guides had set up our camp for us by the time we arrived. One of the highlights of our campsite was Tent #1. As privileged as it seems, my father had spent extra money on an extra porter and a portable toilet just for us—and it turned out to be the best money he could have ever spent.

It's a bucket-list thing

Chapter 2
WELCOME TO MY BUCKET LIST

VERN

Ever had a daydream you couldn't shake? One that happened over and over? I'm not talking about a nightmare, but a daydream where your mind wanders to a place or an experience that is so vivid, you can physically feel it with your senses, even though you have never actually been there.

Since around age eight, I have daydreamed about climbing Mt. Kilimanjaro. While some may think it is from my bucket list, it is more than that for me. I have imagined the smell of the rainforest, heard the calls of the monkeys, and listened to the chatter of the porters guiding climbers up the shale-covered trail to the summit.

In retrospect, it seems strange that I developed a passion for Kili at such an early age.

Here's how it began.

While I was growing up, my father worked days as a tractor mechanic and helped my grandfather with chores in the evenings and on weekends. We lived on a family farm, where we raised cattle, chickens, and hogs for meat, while maintaining a large vegetable garden. We were never hungry, though I'm pretty sure we consumed animal parts most would never consider eating. I thought I hated cheese until my first year of college, because the only "cheese" we ever ate was headcheese—which is as far removed from dairy products as one can get.

We were raised by parents who enforced the clean-your-plate rule. That was not typically a problem because I loved fruits and vegetables, and even pork chops, hamburger, and steaks, although they came from the same animals I played with. The problem with the clean-your-plate rule arose when strange body parts and animal organs were served. Because my father decided each child's appropriate portions, I had no choice but to eat it. Early on, I learned to reach for the ketchup and mustard to disguise the disgusting flavors.

In the late 1950s and the early '60s, it was common for grocery stores to run promotions, giving away items based on the amount of food one purchased. When I was around age eight, our local store decided to give away a set of encyclopedias—one volume per week.

While this worked well for some families, it didn't for us, since we seldom needed to purchase much food. And when we did, it usually wasn't enough to qualify for a book. Fortunately for me, they always gave the first volume away with no minimum purchase. As a result, our set of encyclopedias consisted only of volumes A, E, M, and PQ (which were combined, due to the dearth of letter Q topics).

Two lions making their way across the Ngorongoro Crater

I was, and continue to be, a prolific reader. My parents were not. Other than the Bible, the only books around our house were those my sister and I borrowed from the library. Even though our encyclopedia was limited to a few letters, they still offered a wealth of knowledge. This served me well during the age of trivia games, as long as the topic began with one of the letters we owned.

That first volume was a godsend to me. It allowed me to become knowledgeable in all things beginning in the letter "A," from aardvark to azimuth—including Alaska, anal diseases, Argentina, Antarctica, antiseptics, and, of course, Africa. While the penguins of Antarctica were interesting and the polar bears of Alaska unique, two entries grabbed my attention—the mysterious continents of Australia and Africa. Though I had not yet become a diver, the idea of exploring the Great Barrier Reef, encountering the great white sharks, and observing the unique and diverse mammal population was enticing.

But it was Africa that became my obsession. The "Dark Continent" was fascinating, with its massive deserts of the north, the jungle and ape-filled equatorial region, and the diamond-rich southern tip, occupied by the British. I was absolutely mesmerized by the massive savanna in the eastern part of the continent, home to the majestic African elephant, the big cats, the brightly dressed Maasai tribes, and the annual Great Wildebeest Migration, with its millions of wildebeests and zebras. All of which combine to form the perfect foreground to the largest freestanding mountain in the world, Mt. Kilimanjaro.

In spite of the fact that I didn't have the money to travel the thirty miles to Grand Rapids, I routinely daydreamed of navigating the

One of the countless wildebeests in Northern Tanzania

ocean to visit the mystical mountain. Though some suggested the mountain was becoming an obsession, it never dominated my every waking moment. Instead, climbing Kili was something that I simply had to do—sometime. And sometimes, out of the blue, my thoughts drifted to Kili.

Looking back, I'm surprised that I didn't make the trip to Kili earlier. However, there were many more important things requiring my energy. School, finding a job, changing jobs, getting married, having children, starting my first company, finding employees, supporting our children in their studies and sporting events, numerous knee surgeries, navigating a divorce, meeting and marrying Irene, bilateral knee replacements, our son's marriage, followed by those of our four daughters, and finally grandchildren. All of those things were more important than my daydream, even though it occasionally stopped by to visit, as if to say, "I'm still waiting for you."

In our twenty years together, Irene, more than anyone, understood the importance of me making the climb. When she helped me through my rehabilitation following knee replacements, she used Kili to motivate me. When we met our financial advisor for the first time, he asked us what the first item on our "dream list" was, and Irene immediately responded, "For Vern to climb Mt. Kilimanjaro."

For me, Irene's response is a much deeper reflection of who she is as both a life partner and individually, as her own person. While there are many wonderful places we have journeyed together, and many more in our plans, she said, "our" dream was for me to fulfill my dream. She not only supported me, she embraced my dream and made it her dream as well.

But, why now?

Even though I like hiking and cross-country skiing in our beautiful Michigan forests, it's nice to be able to go someplace warm and enjoy the sunshine, so Irene and I spend a part of the winter in the Florida Keys. It is there where I typically do much of my writing and reading.

During our 2013 trip, twice I had thoughts of Kili. Once, while on the paddleboard, the wind gusted as I was battling a wave, causing my knee to twist to the point of becoming painful. As I regained my balance, I wondered how much longer my knees would last. Nineteen years prior to that, at the time of my first replacement, I was told the average lifespan for artificial knees was twelve to thirteen years. Though I was younger and more physically fit than the average knee-replacement patient and was confident mine would last longer, as I paddled along the Atlantic shoreline, thoughts of Kili washed over me when I began experiencing some slight pain. Time to make the climb was running out.

Then, a few days later, while I browsed one of my favorite science websites, a picture of Kili caught my attention. The article talked about the melting of the Kilimanjaro glaciers. Mt. Kilimanjaro without ice fields would not be the same. In my mind's eye, the view of the Northern Ice Field Hemingway wrote about in his essay "The Snows of Kilimanjaro" was part of the experience I wanted. How could it be *my* Kili if there were no glaciers? I was sixty-one, funding was not an issue, and it was time to set a date with an old girlfriend.

Following my morning paddle boarding, which Irene often refers to as my water-boarding (perhaps a Freudian slip, based on my constant struggle to fight the waves on windy days, fearing that I might drown

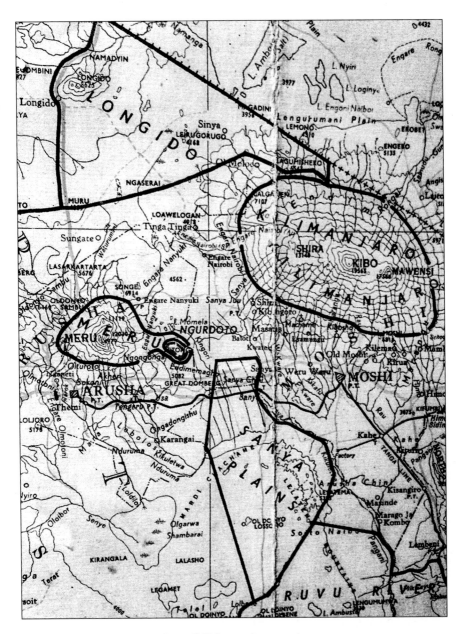

Map of Kilimanjaro region

Waterbuck

or get eaten by one of the sharks I often see), I carried my board up to the beach chairs, where she was enjoying the morning sun. I remember sitting on the end of her chair and saying, "Honey, I have to climb Kili now." Without hesitation, she looked directly into my eyes and said, "Then do it."

After we hugged and kissed, she had some questions.

How long would it take to plan the climb?

Good question, I had no clue. And I certainly needed time to get into better shape. Conditioning for the seven-day climb at unbelievable altitudes is much different than hiking with Irene and our dog Mika through the Michigan ravines or walking while playing thirty-six holes of golf in a day.

In addition, I wanted to invite all of our five children and spouses to climb with me. This would definitely require time and involve them getting two-week vacations, getting into climbing condition, and, in some cases, finding a babysitter.

"Which of the kids do you think will join you?" Irene asked.

An excellent question. All of our kids are extremely active, working out most days, and they are all very competitive. I started with the easiest answer, "Well, you know Kati won't."

Kati is my oldest daughter. She is very fit and exercises regularly. Together with her husband, Jim, they have three children between the ages of four and eleven. But Kati is much like Irene, in that she would consider sleeping in a tent without a shower the equivalent of mental and physical torture. Another issue for her is that she is put off by nearly everything in nature: bugs, animals, birds, fish, and even water that is not encased in cement and connected to a filter. Kati was a definite no; however, her husband, Jim, was a possibility.

My son Adam, and his wife, Hilary, are very athletic. Their three children, ages nine to seventeen, are involved in sports. Adam has always told me that he would join in the climb—however, there was always a small hesitation in his voice. I knew one of the biggest obstacles was his fear of snakes—any and every snake. And I was pretty sure there were a lot of snakes in Tanzania. We established the early betting line, with Adam being a strong favorite to go. In addition, I was confident that if it were simply a safari, Hilary would be in. However, the idea of being filthy and uncomfortable for seven days might tip the scales in the other direction—Irene and I both agreed she was a "maybe."

My daughter Jill and her husband, Ryan, are very much like me in how they approach life. "It sounds like an adventure, and I've got nothing else planned, so let's do it." Besides, Jill has a dream climb of her own. They live in Seattle, and she claims that Mt. Rainier has been calling out to her. Where does she get that silliness? Their willingness was never in question. The only possible problem was that Jill and Ryan both just changed careers in preparation for starting a family. They might not want to delay their family for another couple years, plus getting two-week vacations might be a challenge. Still, I put them both in the "yes" category. I had no doubt they would make it happen.

Irene's daughter Julie and her husband, Justin, are fitness enthusiasts. Both are in excellent condition. They have two children, ages nine and ten, and, as you might guess, are both very active. We agreed there was a pretty good likelihood they would join in. The only significant obstacle was that Julie had never been away from her children for more than a couple of days. She is a work-at-home mom and is very engaged with their school and activities. On the positive side, because they live close by, Irene would be available to care for their children.

Kristin, Irene's youngest daughter, and her husband, Andy, are also involved in a regular exercise routine and typically up for any challenge. (I wonder if this competitive streak is due to nurture or nature?) We both believe there is a good chance they will be joining us. After all, Kristin loves animals, and the safari would be a strong draw for her, though she would need to overcome her dislike of sleeping in tents and being dirty for a week. Andy is very adventurous, and I think he will love to go, but only if Kristin is in.

Our best guess was there would be anywhere from three to as many as nine. Regardless of the number, it was time to get the ball rolling. That day I began my research.

It has been our practice the last eleven years to invite all of the kids and their families for a week-long vacation during Thanksgiving week. Irene does extensive research to find a four- to five-bedroom home, typically in the Caribbean or Central America. The children pay for their transportation to the location, and Irene and I assume the other expenses. They are very active vacations and include golf, hiking, scuba diving, fishing, boating, and so on. Evenings are typically filled with some type of competition, such as cards, trivia, or board games. To get the vacations rolling, Irene emails an invitation to each of the kids in late February or early March to determine the size of the house and the vehicle required.

This year, however, the invitation would come from me. After doing nearly a month of research, visiting numerous websites, and reading an assortment of blogs from climbers, I had to write the email. My hands trembled and the tears flowed as I composed the message. On February 27, 2013, my email began:

As I think most of you know, I have a relatively short bucket list. Now that I have found the one person I want to spend the rest of my life with, there are only three things left. Number one is to climb Mt. Kilimanjaro. Now that I'm sixty and my knees are beyond their normal life expectancy, it is time.

In late July or early August, I will be traveling to Tanzania to climb Mt. Kilimanjaro. I am inviting all our children and their spouses to join me. Even though Irene wishes me well, she has no interest in making the trip, the climb, or living in a tent for a couple weeks. I completely understand. The trip I have been most impressed with includes a seven-day climb and four days on safari.

Following our normal family vacation programs, we will pay for all costs while in Africa.

Climbing in July or August of 2014 will give everyone seventeen months to prepare for the trip.

I then addressed a very serious issue regarding groups climbing together.

What happens if I cannot continue the climb? Does someone stay back and descend with me, or do the other climbers continue their challenge? Or a more personal concern that most can relate to: What happens if someone is unable to continue? Will the spouse continue the climb?

I decided that this issue needed to be addressed early on, rather than dealing with it on the side of the mountain. If this could cause a divorce or physical harm to a spouse, we needed to clarify our intentions before we started.

Before anyone makes any quick or harsh judgments, it is important to understand that the person descending is not left to his or her own devices to get back. Each group that climbs is required to hire a sufficient number of guides and porters to match the number of climbers and the gear transported. In the event that someone must descend, that person would be transported back to the resort by one of the guides and as many porters as required, to await the return of the rest of the group once they complete the climb.

Elephants in the Ngorongoro Crater

I struggled with that scenario for several days, understanding how someone might feel betrayed if a spouse or a family member did not accompany him or her. In addition, I also knew how difficult it would be to get into the physical condition required for the climb. It was also important to realize that few get an opportunity to climb Kili once. To get there and not do everything possible to reach the summit would haunt us for the rest of our lives. I also knew that our children are very strong-willed, independent, and capable of making this commitment.

I decided to add the following message:

Unique to this trip, there are three small exceptions: I'll pay for these costs for everyone that climbs at least as far as I do. That shouldn't be a problem for you kids. Second, knowing how competitive we all are, if anyone injures me or otherwise intentionally impedes my progress—no money for you! Finally, if anyone is unable to proceed up the mountain, everyone else is expected to continue. This is a once-in-a-lifetime opportunity, and if I couldn't make it, I would insist on the rest of you completing the climb.

I hope you will consider joining me on this unique journey.

The kids immediately recognized that the non-payment was a bluff, as I was making the payments prior to departure and I would never ask them to repay me. It did, however, make a statement that all who were joining us were there primarily for the climb. The safari was merely a reward for taking on the challenge. In addition, they all instinctively understood that it would be embarrassing if a sixty-two-year-old out-climbed them and made it to the summit. If they didn't, this fact would undoubtedly surface at nearly every family outing for as long as any of us were alive to tell the story. There was no doubt that anyone joining us would make certain to be physically and mentally prepared for the challenge.

As I pushed "send" and heard my invitation whoosh out into the Web, tears of joy fell to the keyboard. *Kili, I hope you have room. I'm coming for a visit.*

Who's In?

For some reason, as wonderful as our children are, most of them are horrible at responding to emails in a timely manner. They may be on Facebook numerous times a day, so I know they continually visit their electronic devices. However, getting a response from a simple e-mail is like teaching a fish to walk. With this e-mail, I was confident it would be different. I would have bet a lot of money that we would receive responses from all of the kids within a couple of days. After all, this was far too important to overlook.

Within fourteen minutes, Julie was the first to respond, "Ooh, things just got interesting." No commitment, but the message definitely had its desired impact.

Jill was the first to jump in feet first. Within five hours, she enthusiastically responded, "I want to climb a mountain!" I knew it. That's my girl. Ten hours later Adam checked in with: "Me too! It sounds like I better get my ass in gear and get working out." Awesome.

Julie and Justin were the next to respond, though with a little bit more caution; "Wow, thank you. We are seriously considering this. It was all we could think about while trying to fall asleep last night—we were pretty wired. :) Two weeks is such a long time, though." She then questioned the additional time for the safari, and I explained that they could leave after the climb but that I was rewarding myself with a safari and a great resort. Julie is obviously Irene's daughter—cautious and logical.

Within seconds, Irene responded with a very predictable; "If you decide to go, I get your kids!"

Ryan, the most recent addition to our family, hedged Jill's immediate response with an uncharacteristic: "Vern, you've outdone yourself once again ;-) This sounds amazing. Jilly and I will have to discuss." I didn't expect the caution coming from Ryan, but it made sense with everything they had going on in their lives.

Mother baboon feeding her baby alongside the road

After fewer than twelve hours, we had one "yes," two "maybes," and two "seriously considering." Not bad.

Since I didn't hear from Kati, I called to ask. As we predicted, she had no interest, and Jim would not be able to join us either. Kristin and Andy did consider the offer, but as they were trying to start a family, they decided against the climb. I knew it wasn't for everyone, and only those who shared the dream should attempt a climb of such difficulty.

I then began to solidify the plans for our adventure by collecting information about the various routes and the gear. With each inquiry, I would copy all of the kids in an obvious attempt to entice them to join me and solidify each commitment.

As with any adventure, my first notion was to gather as much information as possible from a variety of sources. Eight years ago, a business friend from Detroit told me of her family trip to climb Mt. Kilimanjaro. I had spoken to her about my own desire to climb and asked her numerous times to describe their experience.

Lisa was in excellent physical condition—in her early thirties at the time—and had successfully completed a series of marathons, including Boston. She explained how her Kili climb was the most difficult thing she had ever accomplished and educated me on the physical and mental challenges. Interestingly, her eyes and facial expressions conveyed an even more powerful message: "You don't have a clue." She went on to describe in detailed response suggestions regarding the route to take, the climbing company to hire, and preparations to make. She also volunteered to respond to any questions my children might have, specifically from the girls.

Though petite in size, Lisa is meticulous about her appearance, seemingly never with a hair out of place and dressed in the latest fashions. Her first advice to the girls, "You will be the dirtiest you have ever been in your life and smell worse than you ever thought possible. There are no toilet facilities, you will be miserable for the first six days, but then you will summit and experience something unlike anything you dreamt possible."

Irene and I have been fortunate to travel extensively throughout the world and rarely use a travel agency, so we can explore on our own without a schedule.

This trip was totally different. We would be arriving in Kilimanjaro after dark, without knowing who we could trust to rent an automobile. Trying to coordinate lodging, guides, transportation, the climb, and the safari was well beyond my comfort zone. Lisa recommended the travel agency that her parents used on their frequent trips to Africa. I am certain there are a lot of very competent agents who could book a trip of this nature, but I felt especially grateful that the agent I used had summited Kili ten months before. The travel agent recommended the same climbing company she'd used because of her own experience with them.

In addition to taking advantage of Lisa's knowledge, I searched websites for blogs, videos, and advice from tour operators on what to pack, how to pack, and the route to climb.

There are some incredibly helpful sites that are very specific regarding the recommended gear. And nearly all agreed that the first purchase should be hiking boots. More important, they were adamant that the boots should be well worn prior to the climb. In fact, one site I visited said that the guides could tell who would succeed by looking at climbers' boots. If the boots were new and shiny, there was virtually no chance for success. One website went so far as to claim that blisters on the feet were one of the top three reasons for a failure to summit.

While I have a couple pair of well-worn and comfortable hiking boots, I was pretty sure there was a significant difference between boots for Kili and those designed for our Michigan hills and ravines. The question: where to find the right boots?

Jill recommended REI. I had no idea who, or what, REI was, prior to her referral. She explained that it was a Seattle-based retailer for outdoor activities, specializing in climbing. REI has an incredible Web-based business, as well as numerous stores around the country.

Even though it was the middle of May, a full fifteen months prior to our climb, I was feeling a sense of urgency to buy my boots to ensure they would be completely broken in. I called REI and was referred to its mountain climbing boot specialist. Who would know such a person existed? When I reached him, he wanted to know the mountain I was climbing, as well as the time of year I would be making the climb. I felt like I had definitely called the right place.

Once the boot specialist and I agreed on a boot, he told me that I shouldn't order them over the Internet, due to the size differences between boot manufacturers. Being skeptical of salespeople, I explained that I had worn a size ten for forty years. Wouldn't that be a logical place to start? After ten minutes of explanation about how boots are made and how shoe manufacturers' sizes vary, he pleaded, "You need to try on the specific boots with various layers of socks that you will need for the climb. To do that, you really need to come into our store and try them on."

"Okay, where is your nearest store?"

It turned out they had a couple of stores in Michigan, the closest about three hours away. Irene and I are always up for a road trip, so we scheduled a trip to Ann Arbor for some boot shopping for me, along with a trip to a wine bar and a restaurant as an enticement and a reward for Irene's assistance.

Unfortunately, the store did not keep the model of boot I had selected in stock. But it did have a similar boot made by the same company, La Sportiva. The salesperson first helped me select the sock liners and the three pairs of socks I would need for the trip. Only after that did she allow me to try on the boots.

I told her I wore a size ten, but she returned with an eleven, an eleven and a half, and a twelve, explaining, "I think we should start with the eleven and a half." Trying to be accommodating, I began slipping into a boot that I was certain would be too large. She then asked something I hadn't heard in at least fifty years: "Do you know how to lace and tie them?"

Though I wondered, *How stupid do you think I am?* I instead said, "If you are asking me that question, my answer is probably, no."

With that, the salesperson patiently showed me a way to lace and tie hiking boots that allowed the heel to be drawn squarely and comfortably into the back of the shoe. This enabled the toes to maintain the proper distance from the front of the shoe during the descent, while keeping

Ostrich and antelope

Lion cubs in Ngorongoro Crater

the ankle loose enough to extend and flex. I am convinced her simple instructions saved me from having blisters.

After watching me walk around the store for several minutes, the salesperson determined size twelve was my optimal size. Just purchasing boots made me realize how much I needed to learn prior to making the climb.

Sharing my shopping experience with the kids had exactly the opposite effect I had hoped. Adam began to question if it was something he wanted to do. He was torn because he wanted to share the experience with me but wondered about the physical demands, the cold and the extreme altitude, and, of course, the snakes. His commitment was clearly beginning to waver.

In addition to Adam's apprehensions, Jill and Ryan had concerns about the costs of airline tickets and the gear required, along with those about their jobs and starting a family. That left Julie and Justin, who had yet to commit.

It was mid-June, and we would be leaving on the trip in a year. I had contacted the travel agency, the guide group, and our lodgings and had begun purchasing my climbing gear. Now, all I lacked were my climbing companions.

While enjoying a glass of wine and a beautiful sunset over the lake, Irene startled me with this proclamation: "If none of the kids agree to go, I'll climb the mountain with you. I will hate every minute, but I won't let you go alone."

I assured her that if the kids didn't go, I would join a group of climbers to keep from climbing alone. She promptly dismissed the idea, insisting if nobody from the family joined me, she would go. Though not certain of many things, I knew it could never come to having Irene join me. Immediately, I began formulating a plan to make the trip more attractive to everyone.

Though all of the kids are doing quite well in their careers, I realized investing a couple thousand dollars on the airfare, in addition to the money required to purchase climbing gear, would strain their finances.

A couple of days later, I sent another email. The first part told of Irene's declaration, which needed no explanation since everyone knew she wasn't bluffing. I ended by saying we would increase the amount Irene and I would contribute. It was very evident to everyone that I had resorted to begging.

But it worked. Within a couple of days, Julie and Justin said they were definitely in, and during our visit to Seattle, Jill and Ryan also committed to the trip. Adam and Hilary fluctuated back and forth until January 2014, before deciding that the journey was not something that they would love doing.

It was official: there would be five in the Jones party for a date with Kili.

JUSTIN

I knew the trip had been in the works for more than five years when, over drinks, Vern mentioned a mountain in Africa he'd always wanted to conquer. Even back then, I could tell Vern knew his window for climbing Mt. Kilimanjaro was closing in on him.

It was a sunny summer day, and we were looking out over the lake behind Vern and Irene's house. Vern and I were talking about adventures we would someday like to take. Vern doesn't talk about trips where you simply pack your bags and go. His trips usually involve a lot of activity and a significant amount of planning. Granted, because of Vern's love of golf, most of the trips we took were about golfing. Then, all of a sudden, Vern changed the conversation saying, "I want to go to Africa and climb Mt. Kilimanjaro." That definitely caught me by surprise.

When the invitation arrived, it was apparent he needed people to commit. I think Vern knew I wanted to go and that maybe if he could get me to commit, he would have at least one person ready to join him. However, the trip was two weeks long, and my wife, Julie, and I needed to figure out what to do with the kids, since there was no way I would take the trip without her. One night over dinner and wine, Julie

Vern and Irene

told me she didn't want to be away from the kids for such a long time. As we discussed it, we went back and forth between missing the kids and the chance of taking the trip of a lifetime. The next day our son had a baseball game. Irene and Vern were in attendance. That's when Julie finally told them we were in for the trip.

JULIE

When Vern's invitation arrived by email, Justin and I were sitting in our living room, each of us in our usual positions of relaxation on the couch, checking our phones/iPads and watching television. I read it in shock, then looked over at Justin. "Did you see Vern's email?" He had.

Wow. I never saw that one coming. I hadn't even known that this was something Vern had wanted to do since childhood. My husband and

I are fairly active people and regularly work out together. Even on our honeymoon, we opted out of the more traditional sun/beach/sand location and instead chose a week in Colorado for hiking, horseback riding, and cave explorations. There, we did visit the summit of Pike's Peak, standing at 14,110 feet, but we didn't climb it (and the thought never occurred to me) and instead took the cog train to the top.

Mt. Kilimanjaro is a whole other beast. Standing at 19,341 feet, Kili is so tall, temperatures at the top are cold enough to sustain giant glaciers. And we would not be taking a cozy train to the top, as we did at Pike's Peak. In total, the trip would require a thirteen-day stay in Africa, with seven days of climbing. There would be no bathroom facilities, we'd be in tents, there would be frigid temperatures, and it would be an extremely challenging physical and mental endurance test. It would also include a safari and accommodations at a luxury resort after the climb. I did know that I wanted to live to say I had done it, though I was still on the fence about actually doing it. Add to that the time away from the kids, the expense, being on another continent in a foreign land, the discomfort, and the potential physical pain. These were all factors in my decision. It was a lot of information to take in.

We didn't make a decision right away. But when Vern's second email arrived, we knew it was time to make our choice. I was also worried about my mom saying she would go if we didn't.

A bit of background, which I include with nothing but the utmost respect and love for my mom. She's my best friend, my hero, and the greatest woman I know. She is, however, not what one would call a fan of extremes. She knows what her comfort zone is and loathes straying outside of it. Mom knows her limits and is not afraid to let anyone know what they are. Her imagination, like mine, can run rampant, and I know that she has imagined each of her loved ones in a precarious situation, clinging to life. Late for curfew? I was dead in a ditch. Didn't check in when I said I would? Paralyzed in the ER after some terrible accident.

Over a bottle of Stag's Leap at a Carrabba's Grill, Justin and I conferred and committed.

Yes, we were really doing it.

JILL

The invitation came out of the blue during a slow bar shift, as I was making small talk with the few people left sitting at the bar and checking my email. Opening that email would change my train of thought for the next year and a half. My heart began to race. I have been a hiker for years and could think of nothing more valuable than standing on a mountain-top with my husband and family. Nevertheless, the invitation of a lifetime from my father couldn't have come at a more confusing time.

I had just completed my schooling at a medical institute to change careers from twelve years of bartending to being a physical therapy assistant. It was time to start the next chapter in my life, after working my butt off in my thirties putting myself through college. I was thirty-five years old, married five years to the love of my life, and planning on trying to start a family.

I chose to move away from Michigan and my family when I was twenty years old and kept moving farther and farther away until I hit the West

These boots were meant for climbing

Coast. Although I consider my dad and me to be very close, unfortunately I don't get to hear about his dreams as much as I would like.

When I reached my husband, he was excited about the opportunity. Still, Ryan tends to be a little more grounded than I am when it comes to finances, so he was not convinced it was something we could pull off (not to mention it would completely mess up our family plans). He was right. The math just did not work out. Plus, I was about to get my first job as an outpatient physical therapy assistant, and we both agreed we were going to start trying to have a baby in eight months. In addition, Ryan had recently started a new job he loved. Things were starting to fall in place.

When spring hit in Seattle, and the snow started to melt in the mountains, my hiking buddy Meghan and I had started hitting the trails every weekend. She and I have been on upwards of fifty hikes over the years. Africa was without a doubt a reoccurring topic on many of our hikes, and for once, the trip was actually a possibility. The more time I spent outdoors, the more it began to seem attainable and something I wanted to do. I figured if we were going to wait until 2014 to try for a baby, why not hold off until after the climb? I started coming home from my hikes and telling Ryan all about the adventures, while discreetly mentioning how fun and amazing it would be to go to Africa.

That fall, my dad and Irene decided to come for a visit. One night during dinner my dad started putting the pressure on for us to commit one way or another. The financial worry was the one thing that kept us from saying we were in. Although Vern has always been more than generous when it comes to funding vacations (and this one would be no exception), it was still going to be a stretch for us to afford. Not only would we be responsible for our flights, but the gear we would have to buy would most certainly add up quickly. The dinner conversation turned to work and business-related topics, when Vern saw an opportunity for Ryan to help his business out. Vern then offered to pay Ryan for his work, as long as the money was going to be used to help us buy tickets to Tanzania. I could not have been happier. We were in!

RYAN

A typical Jones family vacation usually kicks off with an email letting us kids know where we're going, followed by a sentence or two about how the same deal applies as previous years.

The "deal," as Vern calls it, consists of each couple paying for transportation to said destination. Once there, everything else is taken care of: housing, food, drink, and excursions (i.e., scuba, golf, day trips, etc.). It's amazing, and I can't thank him enough.

With Jill's family all traveling from Michigan, most destinations are focused on the Caribbean region, such as Puerto Rico (where Jill and I eventually were married), the Dominican Republic, or, a family favorite, the Mayan Riviera. Most of these trips are over the Thanksgiving week to allow family members the opportunity to take advantage of the shorter work week.

For several years, Jill had said something about Mt. Kilimanjaro and how that's something Vern always wanted to do. He had even considered making it an official family vacation. However, at the time it seemed a bit unrealistic and mostly talk. But whenever Vern gets the itch to do something, odds are it will happen.

Ryan and Jill on one of their many adventures

The official invitation sounded pretty sweet and hard to pass up. However, at $5,000 for airfare and dropping a couple thousand more on gear, it didn't seem like something we could handle at that time. Jill and I had recently traveled to Thailand, and I had started a new job about six months prior. Combine that with Jill and me thinking of starting a family, and it seemed unlikely we'd make the trip.

A few months later, when Vern and Irene came to Seattle for a visit, the four of us went out for dinner—which allowed Vern to make one last sales pitch. He knew we were on the fence (which was unusual—most of the time we say yes and ask questions later). Because of the cost, I couldn't say yes. At the same time, we couldn't bear the thought of turning down such an amazing opportunity. What to do, what to do? Then Vern made one final offer, for me to do some consulting work in exchange for some of the costs. Jill and I looked at each other, smiled, and started laughing. I turned back to Vern, "Sounds like a plan. When do I get started?"

IRENE

I was raised to fear just about everything. To name a few: don't walk on the grates of a sidewalk because you could fall through and die; don't drink a can of pop outside because a bee could get in there and sting you while you swallowed it; don't put your arm outside the window because a car could come by and cut it off. But the best, if you see a big dog, run!

Then I met Vern. He showed me a new world. There wasn't anything he wasn't willing to try. From the very beginning, he told me of his dream to climb Mt. Kilimanjaro. That surprised me. I had never met anyone who wanted to do something so adventurous.

Our team

Vern has encouraged me to try many things: snorkeling, diving, riding a horse across the mountains, river rafting in Virginia, water skiing, and snowmobiling through Yellowstone. Some I had success with and others not so much. My rule was, I would try everything once.

When Vern started doing his research on Mt. Kilimanjaro, I knew it wasn't anything I would ever want to try. In the back of my mind, I still didn't think this was going to happen, until the invite letter was sent. My role in the trip would be that of support. I knew I had to be strong. Not just for myself, but for the grandkids, who had never been away from their parents for that long.

BODIN

Hi, my name is Bodin, and I felt sad and happy when my mom and dad and grandpa left for Mt. Kilimanjaro. I was happy because I got to stay with my grandma for two weeks. I was sad because I didn't get to see my mom and my dad for two weeks. When they left, my sister sobbed and my grandma had little tears, and I'm not going to brag or anything, but I didn't show one tear.

REESE

It all started when I woke up sad. We were going to Nama's and Papa's house. We drove. Bodin was happy. I was sad. We got there. Knocked on the door. I got excited! But when they left, I cried. Let me tell you about day one. First, we went to Build-A-Bear workshop. I got Teacup! Next, we went to Chuck E. Cheese's. And I wasn't scared.

Chapter 3
THE PERFECT BALANCE

VERN

I've always enjoyed all types of physical and mental competition—something that has continued into my sixties. In business, I am constantly trying to figure out better ways to organize my businesses and interact with employees. This urge to compete stretches into my personal life, even driving me to need to hit a golf ball better or farther than others.

I credit some of this competitive nature to my brother Doug, who is five years older. Growing up, I constantly tried to convince him and his friends to let me join in their football or basketball games. This was in spite of my lack of size, speed, and strength. The beatings I absorbed whenever I joined them taught me to lose graciously, strive to improve, and savor the rare victories. The first sport where I could compete on an even basis was basketball, which remains my passion to this day.

This competitive nature has served me well, in both my business and my personal life. My son Adam was three when I met his mother—falling in love with both of them. He and I spent endless hours playing tennis and baseball, shooting baskets, and playing golf and

Ping-Pong. A few years later, my daughter Jill was born, and it became obvious that she had a similar competitive fire. We adopted Kati from her home country of Korea when she was seven, and Jill, who was a couple years younger, helped her acclimate to this country.

All three kids became involved in activities that allowed them to test their physical and mental limits. Even though we had a hoop, none of our kids shared my love for basketball. Yet more important, the kids used our friendly competition to develop lifelong habits that resulted in all of them having successful professions that fueled their passions.

Adam was a very good baseball player, whose teams I coached until he entered high school. The girls were interested in softball, and I also coached their teams. Twice, our team went to the Little League World Series.

Vern in 1976 with baby daughter Jill

Though our marriage proved difficult, the kids and their activities kept me focused, which, along with my professional career, kept meaning and joy in my life. Like other marriages that collapse due to years of conflict, things were difficult for the kids—as was the divorce.

After sixteen years of marriage, I wasn't prepared for the dating thing. Soon, I learned that the opposite of past unsuccessful flings was equally bad. After some very bad choices, I informed Jill that I was done with dating. Then, two weeks later, my world changed forever when I asked Irene out on a date.

I had met Irene four years' prior while coaching softball. She was the mother of Julie, who was a player on one of our All-Star teams. As the team traveled to Michigan's Upper Peninsula for the state championship and again for the regional in Illinois, the parents followed along. I was aware that Irene had also recently gone through a divorce. But there was no way in hell that I was going to date, or even socialize with, the parent of a player. During those trips, I completely ignored her, knowing that even the slightest attempt at friendliness would be scrutinized by the parents whose children were not starters. Irene told me later that I appeared arrogant and obnoxious during those trips—which I like to explain is now what she loves about me.

Though skeptical of the term *soul mate*, I do know that after twenty years of marriage, I am flattered that Irene loves me, she is my best friend, and our lives are filled with laughter, love, and respect. In addition, we have five incredible children, along with their families. Life doesn't get any better than this!

JULIE

I've always been a rather anxious person. As a child, there was a time when I could not fall asleep because I was certain our house was going to catch fire. Whenever a severe weather warning hit the news, I assumed a tornado was going to sweep our house away, in spite of living in Michigan where tornados are rare. If I wanted to keep my window open during a hot and muggy night, I thought someone would burst through the screen and steal me away.

Once, when I was in the fifth grade, I hopped on my bike to ride to school, only to discover a ridiculous number of worms sprawled out on our street. I made it past three houses before turning back—gagging and crying—to beg my mom for a ride to school because killing worms with my bike distressed me so much. Once I arrived, my teacher gave me a new nickname—SB for Spoiled Brat.

I despised going into our unfinished basement by myself so much that I coerced my younger sister into being my bodyguard.

My general paranoia was not completely unfounded. One summer, we had an infestation of earwigs in our living room—nasty-looking insects, about one-inch long, with two giant pincers on their rear ends and bodies covered with hard armadillo-like armor. When exterminated by one's shoe, they made a spine-tingling "crunch." One afternoon, while sitting on our couch watching television, I felt something land on the top of my head. When I brushed it off, I recoiled in horror from the realization that it was an earwig. In fact, there were several of them crawling around on our ceiling. Surely the stuff of nightmares.

Julie and Justin at a golf outing

This anxiety has followed me into adulthood. Taking a trip by plane? Leave hours earlier than necessary, so we won't be late. Looking for a new home with two kids under the age of four? Flat-out reject all two-stories because stairs are a death trap for children, and WHY WOULD WE BUY A DEATH TRAP FOR OUR CHILDREN?

I worry about everything, from what I'm going to talk about at a social gathering to how my kids are going to fare at school after I wave

Sisters Kristin and Julie

goodbye to them as they board the bus (also worrying, of course, about their bus driver getting them to school safely).

I need to know where my kids are twenty-four hours a day. When they are at school, I worry about them falling off the monkey bars and breaking their arms. When they are out and about with their Nama and Papa, I hope they are properly restrained in their booster seats and seat belts. When they are outside at home playing with friends, I frequently listen for their spirited laughter and shrieks of indignation at whatever offense one sibling is inflicting on the other. Whenever I hear a yell, I run outside to make sure everything is okay. Or at least that no one is bleeding or has a stubbed toe or a scraped arm.

Surely, other mothers are this paranoid, right?

When Vern sent the invite about climbing Mt. Kilimanjaro, I was less worried about the physical aspects of the climb and more concerned about leaving our kids behind for two weeks. For the last nine years, I had not spent more than two nights in a row away from them. I didn't know how I would handle things, and, for reasons unexplained, I felt as though I was abandoning them—even though I knew I would be leaving them in the care of my mom.

I have never been an outdoors person. The last time we slept in a tent was two years ago in our suburban backyard. And it was epic. Justin didn't realize he had set up the tent on top of our neighbor's sprinklers, which were set to go off at four in the morning. The chick-chick-chick sound instantly woke me up from a surprisingly sound sleep, and moments later, our non-waterproof tent was covered in an unrelenting surge of water. We all got soaked and ran back into the house, yelling and hysterically laughing at the same time. The thought of sleeping in a tent perched on the side of a mountain in Africa, with no flushing toilets or running water, was daunting.

I have been physically active my entire life. This included playing multiple sports in high school, playing softball in college, and maintaining a regular workout schedule at home with my husband. Though I knew I could get fit enough to make the climb, I was concerned about things that were out of my control, like an injury, the altitude, or traveling—for the first time—to another continent.

But, I'm also adventurous and knew this was something I wanted to do. Kili, here I come!

JUSTIN

Growing up, I was trouble for my parents and, to this day, feel bad for being such a shit. At the same time, I was voted the sweetest person in my class.

How many people can say they were in a Dodge Ram when it went into a lake? Granted, it was not the entire truck—the two back wheels were still on dry land. However, the severe drop-off did put the entire front end up to the windshield underwater. I actually saw fish swim past the headlights, prior to them shorting out.

A lot of my early memories involve altercations. One of my first fights was on a school bus with a bully who liked to pick on younger kids, like me. But the bully picked on the wrong kid. I was big—okay, fat—and when the bully decided to call me Hungry Hungry Hurley after the 1970s game Hungry, Hungry Hippos, I warned him to be careful. Instead, he looked at me and said, "Hungry, Hungry, Hurleeerrwr," which he barely finished, prior to me jumping over two bus seats to silence him.

Fast-forward ten years and multiple altercations later to my senior year in high school. I was playing basketball in the biggest game of the year against our rivals, and we were losing badly. I believe we lost by eighteen points. By the end of the game, I was sitting on the bench because I hadn't played well. As the clock wound down, an opposing player threw up a three-pointer, as a tall, slim, and clumsy member of our team tried blocking the shot. When he went up to block, he brushed the player shooting it, who raised his fist against my teammate. Immediately, I was off the bench, resulting in both benches clearing. Later, when my coach suspended me for a game, he said if I'd moved that fast during the game, we might have won. Unfortunately, the entire fight was broadcast on live TV as the local game of the week.

All my life I have disliked people who pick on those unable to defend themselves. I've never started a fight in my life, though I was too quick to throw a punch. That may have been why I was voted the sweetest guy in my high school class.

When Vern asked us to go on the trip, I was ready to take on the bully, Mt. Kilimanjaro.

JILL

I grew up in a small suburban town in West Michigan named Jenison. Its population is largely of Dutch origin and pretty conservative. But our family life was different from the families living around us. My

A young Jill posing for the camera

brother Adam, who's four years older than me, is from my mom's first marriage. Then, when I was five years old, my parents adopted my sister Kati, who is from Korea and two and a half years older than me. Though Jenison has a lot of good points, it is not ethnically diverse. Even though we lived in that environment, my parents did a great job incorporating Kati's Korean culture into her life.

In addition to the Korean influence in our house, one year we welcomed two exchange students from Brazil—brothers Mauro and Aruldo. Though they were from a well-to-do family, initially they spoke very little English. That experience led us to travel to Brazil for a month to visit their family. It was my first plane ride, and, with connections, it took fourteen hours to get there from Michigan. Although I was very young, I enjoyed traveling.

After graduating from high school, I got my first job, as a waitress, which allowed me to afford my own apartment—an independence I cherished.

Even though Michigan was a wonderful place to grow up, I wanted to experience other places. After two years of living in downtown Grand Rapids, I knew it was time to hit the road, and I set my sights on Colorado. My plan was to work in a restaurant during the busy ski season and take the summer off to travel. My dad arranged for me to drive a car out for a friend of his who had a daughter in Aspen. Once there, I would be on my own. However, things didn't quite work out as planned. While I was driving through Minnesota, the car broke down. Though I could have taken it as a bad sign and turned around to go home, instead I got the car fixed and was back on the road in two days.

I managed to make it the rest of the way without incident and dropped off the car. From there, I met up with a girl I'd worked with at the Grand Rapids Brewery, who attended college in Gunnison, Colorado. I got a job at the nearest ski resort, Crested Butte, where I worked seasonally for two years. I loved living among the mountains and in the carefree atmosphere of a ski town. Strangely enough, I never got into skiing, though I loved to snowshoe, hike, and take advantage of the music scene.

After two seasons in Crested Butte, I decided to move somewhere that had more culture, was near the water, yet had mountains.

One of my girlfriends from high school had just graduated from college and wanted to move to the West Coast. Neither of us had seen the Pacific Ocean, and we didn't know anyone there. Our plan was to drive to the coast, camping along the way. We decided to start in San Francisco,

Julie shows off her injured knee

working our way north to Portland and finally Seattle, in order to see which city we liked best. Basically, we ran out of money in Seattle and have now lived there for sixteen years. Although it sounds like I was stranded there, nothing could be further from the truth.

RYAN

I was born and raised in Mission Viejo, California. Growing up in the '80s and the '90s, I spent most of my weekends at the beach, with my local breaks being Strands, Salt Creek, and T-Street in the San Clemente area. We chose beaches based on the surf conditions and whether the break was overhead. One foot of surf could make the difference in whether we made it to school or not. Life was a beach, so they say. I think this is where my carefree spirit began to take shape.

In 1993, I moved to Seattle to attend the University of Washington (Go, Dawgs!). Words can't express my love for the city and passion for the Northwest lifestyle (Have I mentioned I'm a Washington Husky fan?), though the transition from the warm Southern California climate to the milder Northwest wasn't easy at first. Rather than spending time on the beach, in the Northwest it's all about the Olympic and Cascade Mountain ranges, evergreens, and surrounding bodies of water. There is some amazing backcountry less than an hour from the city. In fact, during my freshman year, a friend got me a job giving snowboard lessons at local resorts like Crystal, Stevens, and Mt. Baker, along with world-class conditions four hours away at Whistler and Blackcomb.

In the summer, there is waterskiing and wakeboarding in the heart of Seattle, along with countless places to hike and camp, including Mt. Rainer, Mt. St. Helens, Mt. Bakers, and Mt. Adams.

The Northwest is also where I met Jill.

Game. Set. Match.

Jill and I have been together for twelve years and married for seven. Together, we've had one adventure after another, and there isn't a day that goes by when I don't count my blessings.

IRENE

My mother came to the States from Germany at the age of eighteen, shortly after the war ended, leaving a fiancé behind. She married my father, an unlikely suitor for her because they were as different as night and day. They immediately started a family—three daughters a year apart and then a son ten years later. My mom had so many talents. She could sew, knit, draw, and write and knew how to stretch a dollar. She was also a worrier, always anticipating the worst and never taking risks. That's the trait she passed on to me. I'm the worrier, but, fortunately, she also taught me how to stretch a dollar.

After a job working for the Internal Revenue Service, I became a stay-at-home mom to my two girls—Julie and Kristin. Seeing and holding Julie, I knew I couldn't leave her. The girls were my life, and I put them before everything else. I was very hands-on when they were young, and they were my playmates. The first time a neighborhood friend knocked on our door to see if they could play, I was heartbroken. Who was I going to play with?

We made many sacrifices, but when times got rough, I always managed to find a part-time job to get us through. At one point, I studied hard in order to get a real estate license and then sold homes.

As the girls got older, I knew I had to let go a little. We had just moved into a new neighborhood, which some people called "the Bubble," because it was as if we had a protective shell around us. Nothing bad ever happened, and neighbors looked out for one another. One day, when Julie was six, I arrived home from my part-time job. I was informed by the babysitter that Julie had ridden her bike to a friend's house and would be home by 5:00. The next time I looked at the clock, it was 5:05. Where was Julie? I called the mother at the house where Julie was playing and was told she had left ten minutes earlier. It was 5:10. Where could she be? I alerted all of my neighbors, and we all began to search. I even called the police, because the sooner we started the statewide search, the better. The police officer wanted me

Ryan's high school portrait.

to describe Julie and what she was wearing. All I could think about was that the outfit she had put on in the morning might be the last one I would ever see her in. The police told me they would be sending someone over, but I continued to search on my own. Then, while talking to a neighbor, I looked down the road. There was Julie riding her bike as if she didn't have a care in the world. I like to think that my reaction, and the subsequent grounding she received, is the reason both of my girls are rarely late.

After my eighteen years of marriage, a divorce changed me—as I'm sure it does everyone. I started to take control of my life. I knew I didn't want to end up like my relatives from the old country, because they were always looking back—some even wishing they had never left Germany.

In a way, I divorced my family, too. I needed to do things my way. I fought to get a job as a sales rep, which came with a company car. It was perfect timing, allowing me to turn our family car over to Julie, who was turning sixteen. I had a savings account and started a 401k account. For the first time in my life, I felt like an adult. I could do everything on my own. With the help of my neighbor, along with Julie and Kristin, we even re-shingled the roof of our house. I was unstoppable. What else could I do?

Five years after my divorce, I met and married the man of my dreams, the person I will grow old with. We are a perfect balance. I can't wait to see what each day brings. Life has never been this exciting.

Chapter 4
POLE-POLE – SLOWLY-SLOWLY
Wednesday, August 6

Day 2: Machame Camp to Shira Camp

VERN

After our first day on the mountain (and due to our late start that day), we had gotten used to climbing at a brisk pace. That night, during our nightly briefing, Philemon repeatedly urged us to slow down our pace. He talked about altitude sickness and how deadly it is. It is the number-one reason climbers fail to summit, and Philemon wanted us all to make it. Our second-day climb would be at a slower pace, with each of us expected to drink our entire three-liter water supply prior to arriving at Shira Camp, our destination.

With morning light, we finally met our entire climbing party, consisting of three guides, a cook, and twenty porters assigned to carry our provisions. Early that morning came a tap on my tent by Kennedy, who was waiting with a cup of hot tea, which was a very

Ready to begin Day 2 climb

nice touch. Moments later, he brought a bowl of warm water so we could freshen up before breakfast. We then packed our daypack and primary packs, and placed them outside the mess tent, so the porters could break down the camp while we enjoyed our warm breakfast and hot tea.

Our discussion centered on our exhilaration on the first day and Julie's knee, which was still aggravated. We hoped our climb that day, which was steep and expected to take approximately six hours, would not be too difficult. Since we were leaving at 8:30, we had the luxury—and the strict instructions from our guide—to hike *pole-pole* (pronounced pole-ay-pole-ay), which means "slowly-slowly."

While much of the first day's climb was on a well-groomed trail, from our camp to the next stop our trail was nonexistent. To navigate, we relied on the experience of our guides to get us around steep rock faces, while being careful not to get injured. All the while, our porters were jogging past us, leaping from rock to rock, carrying our provisions. Their gracefulness was amazing. Here I was using walking poles and wearing $300 boots, while our porters were wearing five-year-old canvas tennis shoes and literally racing past us.

In a lull in our daily chatter, Jill was overcome by a sneezing episode. Sunday informed us that the Maasai believe when you sneeze, someone is thinking about you.

All of our three guides had very different personalities. Sunday was personable and outgoing. He was fond of teaching us Swahili phrases, which we enjoyed learning, especially during the first couple of days, with their long and strenuous stretches. Philemon, our head guide, was very quiet and deliberate. However, on occasion, he would break out of his shell to show a less rigid side. Emmanuel seemed to be the sincerest of the three. Conversations with him were on a much more personal level.

Our pace on our second day was very *pole-pole,* as Sunday brilliantly assisted Julie over the treacherous terrain. However, that significantly stretched out the time required for the six-hour climb. Finally, after climbing for hours, we rounded a rock formation and were greeted with our first view of Kibo—the highest of Mt. Kilimanjaro's three peaks—home of Uhuru, our ultimate destination. As we stopped for a much-deserved break, Philemon, Emmanuel, and Sunday gathered for a conference. We entertained ourselves watching Jill, as she attempted to toss nuts into Ryan's mouth from several feet away.

Our guide Emmanuel

After their discussion, they presented us with what they thought was a viable option. Since Julie was slowing the progress of the group, they suggested that Philemon travel with Julie and Justin, while the rest of us proceed to the camp and begin preparations for dinner. That didn't work for me. I explained that though we appreciated the offer, we were family, not merely a climbing group. Everyone agreed with me, and to show solidarity, we decided to let Julie lead our group, so she could establish a pace that was tolerable.

When we finally arrived at Shira Camp, it was still well before sunset. Even though we were completely exhausted, our view that night was awesome. To the south was the glacier-covered Kibo with its glistening ice fields that changed colors as the sun set, and to the north was a very steep cliff above an amazing sea of gently rolling clouds stretching as far as the eye could see. Standing proudly in the middle of our view was Mt. Meru at slightly over 14,000 feet.

At our altitude that night of 12,500 feet, it was common for climbers to begin experiencing symptoms of altitude sickness. Fortunately, the hypoxic tent I'd rented for the forty-five days prior to leaving paid off. Sleeping and exercising in it resulted in my feeling very comfortable, in spite of the slight oxygen deprivation.

My other training device, the Fitbit, continued to give me valuable information. That morning, the tracker indicated that during Day 1 I had climbed the equivalent of 178 flights of stairs. It challenged me to try to reach 200. On Day 2, as I got ready for bed, it showed I had climbed the equivalent of 602 flights of stairs. Next challenge?

During the day, we progressively took off layers of clothes, as the mid-day temperature reached the high 50s. But the nights were incredibly cold, and the Park Service does not permit fires on the mountain. That eliminated any notion of sitting around a campfire, sharing stories or singing camp songs.

One good decision I made was purchasing a SIM card for Tanzania, which allowed me to call home to talk with Irene almost every night. On our second night, the best reception was near the edge of the mountain, close to the outhouses, not the most pleasant place to be. Having been raised on a farm, I spent nearly every day of my childhood either sloshing through or shoveling animal manure. But I don't recall our barns ever smelling that foul.

My daily conversations with Irene were magical. Speaking with her kept me grounded, reminded me to be safe, and gave me additional motivation. It was hard being away from Irene not only for the length of time I was gone, but because she wasn't with me to share this extraordinary adventure. These daily calls kept her intimately involved and an important part of the endeavor.

Following dinner, the guides measured our pulses and the oxygen concentration in our blood. We were then briefed on the next day's climb, the gear to pack in our daypacks, and the clothes we should wear. Afterward, we went back to our tents, changed into clothes for the next day, and got into our sleeping bags with the clothes we'd worn that day tucked around us, inside our sleeping bags, to dry them out and provide much-needed additional warmth.

Our guide Sunday

Ryan and Jill chucking peanuts at each other

Stacked lava rocks with Kibo awaiting us in the distance

Our second night was very cold. Living in Michigan and raised in a home without heat in the bedrooms, I thought I was prepared for it. I was wrong. On this night, I pulled my buff over my face and wore my gloves to bed.

JULIE

After arriving at camp the previous evening and falling asleep just under the tree line and under cloud cover, we awoke to a bright and sunny day. When we looked toward where our trail upward began, we could see a very tall ridge and beyond that, finally, a fleeting glimpse of the top of Kili! The moment was short-lived, however, as cloud cover once again obscured our view of the mountain.

As we emerged from our tents after brushing our teeth and washing up, using "wash, wash" (warm water placed outside our tents in bowls), I limped over to breakfast, which was being served in an army-green tent that doubled as the porters' sleeping quarters. Much to my relief, my knee felt a whole lot better after a night of rest—though by no means full strength. The agonizing throbbing had ceased, and I could hobble around without too much concern.

After hours of walking through a dense rainforest the day before, we were all ready for some vistas. As we emerged above the tree line on a trail covered with big boulders that we had to actually climb, we got what we'd asked for. The views from start to finish that day were just incredible. An hour into our climb, we were above the clouds and able to see Mt. Meru poking up through the thick and rolling cloud cover in the distance. The flora was lush and green with some interesting and unusual flowers, including the Kniphofia, commonly called the red-hot poker.

On the second day, the trail became more challenging, as pockets of firm, densely packed, flat ground gave way to boulders so large and flat that I had to walk up them in a side-step fashion. Soon, I could no longer fully straighten or bend my right knee. This made climbing up and down the rocks particularly difficult and painful (and slow!).

Our guide Sunday noticed me babying it and urged me to bend it and keep it loose. But whenever I stepped wrong, hot pain snaked up the inside of my leg, causing a flash of tears I could not control. I'd then go back to walking my way, and he'd call me out once again. At one point, I told him I simply could not bend my leg and that if I were going to make it to camp, I'd have to walk my way. The distance from Machame Camp to Shira Camp is just over three miles, though the signpost (and our itinerary) advised us that it would take approximately four hours. As with many signposts during the next couple of days, we blew their expectations out of the water, but not in a good way. We had been hiking for at least five hours when we reached a tall point within the enormous valley and stopped for a snack and a rest.

At this point, our guides met to discuss having Justin and me follow the rest of the group. I was pleased when they refused to go ahead without us.

Because we had rested at a very high point on the trail, we had to backtrack down before we made the push up the ridge that would eventually lead us to camp. Going down sucked almost as much

The sun over Uhuru Peak in the distance

Vern and Jill, Day 2 climb

energy as going up. Sunday, our guide, had made me walk directly behind him, starting that day, and then behind every guide for the rest of the trip. This was for a couple of reasons: first, so he could direct my steps. He would come to a challenging crop of rocks, evaluate them, and then turn to me, point, and say, "Left foot there. Then right foot. Then your left foot goes there." He would often grab my arm and haul me up the last step of a steep cluster of rocks, and then we'd continue on until we came to the next tough spot and start all over again.

It was exhausting, mentally and physically. I was climbing this mountain with my entire body, from my brain and eyes down to the tips of my toes, and including my arms. The second reason my place in line was always behind the guide was to set the pace for the group. Through no fault of their own, when other members of the group were in front of me, they'd naturally walk faster at a clip they

Emmanuel, Philemon, and Ryan above the clouds

Justin, Philemon, Jill, Ryan, and Vern, taking a break

were comfortable with, leaving me behind at my slug's pace. So I became the group's governor, slowing us all down in places when we all wanted to cruise just a little bit faster.

There was still daylight when we arrived at camp, and we were lucky to have some of the cloud cover move out, allowing us the extreme pleasure of viewing a Shira sunset, which was spectacular.

I didn't know this, but Mt. Kilimanjaro is made up of three summits (which are actually three separate volcanic cones), even though many think of the iconic, flat, snow-covered summit when it comes to Kili. The flat-topped dome (with a large crater in the middle) is actually Kibo Summit, which is the highest of the three peaks, and upon which our destination of Uhuru Peak (at 19,341 feet) awaited us. The other two summits are Shira, at 13,000 feet, and Mawenzi, at 16,893 feet. According

Justin and Ryan with Kibo looking down on them

to Wikipedia, Mt. Kilimanjaro is a large stratovolcano, which is also known as a composite volcano. A stratovolcano is a conical volcano built up by many layers (strata) of hardened lava, tephra, pumice, and volcanic ash. Stratovolcanoes are characterized by a steep profile and periodic explosive eruptions and quiet eruptions, although some have collapsed craters called calderas. Of its three peaks, Mawenzi and Shira are extinct, while Kibo is dormant and could erupt again. The last major eruption has been dated between 150,000 and 200,000 years ago.

Aside from the food, the uncomfortable sleeping quarters, and the weather, the Shira sunset was simply amazing. Ryan, Jill, and Vern went on a guided walk around camp—it was that big—to check out caves and stay warm. It was advised that I get off my knee and rest it as much as possible. The trade-off was that I was unable to generate any extra heat by walking around. On went even more articles of clothing than the night before, and into the sleeping bag I went, in hopes of getting some sleep.

JUSTIN

Wow, did I sleep great. I must have been exhausted from the first day's climb because it was cold, and my sleeping bag was made for someone less than six feet tall, which meant I was unable to pull the bag over my shoulders. On top of that, the ground was rock hard.

My first thought on waking up for Day 2 was about Julie's knee. Despite her claims that it felt better, I could feel her concern. Julie thought that if Jill could use tape to give it some support, she would be okay. She couldn't bear the thought of not being able to make it to the top. All I could think about were the books I'd read about focusing on one step at a time.

About two and a half hours into our climb that next day, we got our second glimpse of Kibo. The size of the peak tricked us into thinking it was not that far away. Wrong!

We asked Sunday how much farther we had. "Just over the ridge," he responded. I remember thinking, *I'm good with that.* But an hour later, still no camp. I asked again. "How much farther?" Once more he said, "Just around the corner." It was the beginning of my frustration about the imprecision concerning time and distance. Finally, after nine hours, we arrived at camp.

Over dinner that night, we talked about the day's climb and the sights we'd seen. Later, just prior to bed, the guides measured our pulses and oxygen concentration to make sure we were all fit to climb the next day. It was cold outside, making me wish we had brought along a thermometer. If I had to guess, it was nearing freezing, and it was going to be difficult to stay warm that night.

JILL

On our second morning, I woke to the sound of our ever-attentive waiter Kennedy, smiling as he handed me a hot cup of tea outside my tent. It was early, and there was a brisk chill in the air. But the sun was shining and gave me hope that we would have good weather for a great day of hiking. I sat among bags of clothes scattered along my half of the tent. I strategically placed all my belongings inside my backpack, a routine that would get incredibly familiar as the week progressed.

We made our way to the mess hall for the first breakfast of our adventure. I was hoping for nothing more at this point than for Julie to run up to

Our meal awaits

Ryan and volcanic rock

Vern, Julie, Justin, and Ryan in the lava rock field

Giant goundsels

the tent and say that all she needed was a little rest and she was good to go. Unfortunately, the stiffness in her gait told a different story (as a physical therapy assistant, I watch people walk for a living). I felt terrible about her having pain after only one day, and in most of my experiences, knee pain doesn't go away with more exercise. I offered what little help I could give her with a Kinesio tape and Bio freeze.

We set off for our adventure of Day 2. Although we were still one of the last groups to start, already things seemed to be going smoother than the day before. At this point, we were above the tree line and still surrounded by vegetation. We passed different varieties of flowers. There were tall, slender, delicate mountain gladiolas with burnt red petals that seemed to weep forward. Stalk-like, cone-shaped flowers, appropriately named red hot pokers, ranging from scarlet red to orange to brilliant yellow, nestled within the rocks. The most abundant were the Everlast flowers, which gained their name by surviving in even the driest of climates and are thought to be one of the oldest flower species on earth.

After twenty minutes on the trail, I turned to look back at camp. What once was a bustling city of tents, porters, and travelers from all walks of life now appeared desolate, with only the roofs of outhouses and the registration building marking where we had just been. It was crazy to think in a few short hours that same land would be covered with another city of tents filled with thousands of new faces. I could not believe how hard and fast the porters worked.

This was the hottest day of our hike. As the clouds started to burn off, I got my first site of Kibo. Due to my policy of never being early for anything (some people would call it "late"), I had not seen Kibo in the morning, as some of the more early-rising people in our group had. There it was. The

Jill standing on Kilimanjaro, with Mt. Meru in the background

Julie and Justin, Day 2 climb

glaciers dripped down the side of the mountain, much like candle wax dripping down a sand hill. Though it looked very tall, what surprised me was how far away it looked. Not only were we climbing to great heights, but first we had to climb all the way over to the base.

Soon we were above the clouds and offered a constant view of Mt. Meru. We continued up and up, as our porters, dressed in everything from traditional African clothing to Def Leppard T-shirts, raced by with provisions. Along the way, our enthusiastic guide Sunday continually taught us traditional climbing songs, along with Swahili sayings. When silence happened, which wasn't often, it would be filled with Emmanuel lifting our spirits by singing songs we were more familiar with, like "Everything Is Awesome" from the Lego movie. I wore a pin on the back of my backpack that just said SMILE in block

Vern and one of the many lava boulders on Kilimanjaro

Going down is difficult also

letters. Emmanuel and Sunday took it upon themselves to continually check in and make sure I was following my own instructions.

But we also knew we were way off schedule, due to our pace. We finally came over a ledge and saw Shira Camp. With the sun brightly lighting Kibo, we were able to see the pale blue hue of the glaciers on the right side and the clouds dancing on the horizon with Mt. Meru peeking through a blanket of clouds on our left. This campsite afforded an amazing view in every direction. Julie was able to stand long enough to snap some pictures, though she did need to rest. Although it was clear she was in pain, she would never give up, nor did she complain very much.

While at Shira Camp, Emmanuel led Ryan, Dad, and me to the nearby caves. He explained that in years not so long ago, the area was often covered with snow. The caves provided a place to camp and build fires.

Julie and Jill at Shira Camp

Stepping into a cave, we saw evidence of fires past. It made me happy to have a sleeping bag and a tent, because, even though the snow was long gone, it was still cold. We climbed up to a high point and watched as the sun began to set. Shira Camp is known for its exquisite sunsets, which we witnessed that night. Although I have been on hundreds of hikes over the years, Shira Camp at 12,500 feet provided a view I'd never before seen.

As we investigated our surroundings, we noticed a helicopter pad. We were told that it was the last point along the trip where a helicopter could land. Without pressurized cabins, they were not allowed any higher. Any type of emergency that happened beyond this point required the climber to be carried down to this point or lower, before being airlifted off the mountain. We still had two days of climbing left, not to mention tackling the summit. Though we had paid for Global Rescue Insurance, it didn't mean much after this point.

Jill at Shira Camp, with Uhuru in the background

Our next day involved hiking from Shira Camp (12,500 feet) to Barranco Camp (13,000 feet), with a short stop at Lava Tower, which stands at 15,000 feet, for acclimatization. Total estimated hiking time, according to the signpost/itinerary: 6 to 8 hours to cover 6.2 miles.

Day 3 Thursday, August 7

VERN

During breakfast, we discussed how incredibly cold it became immediately after sunset. Philemon once again talked about hypothermia, stressing the procedures they would use in the event that someone became critically ill. This included him getting naked with the patient in a sleeping bag, surrounded by hot water bottles. In an earlier discussion, Ryan, Justin, and I had joked about this being an option,

On our way to acclimate at Lava Tower

Finding flat land to pitch a tent can be a challenge

if one of us became too lonely. This time, however, we listened more closely—although there were still a few chuckles from time to time.

The landscape resembled a shale-covered savanna littered with huge boulders—some marked with streaks of faded orange paint. Sunday, always a wealth of knowledge, along with his strong philosophical opinions, explained that the marks were painted there to show the path. I asked why they were painted so high on the rocks, at roughly six to eight feet above the ground. He explained that as recently as twenty-five years ago, the camp, now located far below the glaciers, was covered by ice fields. Scientists report that for a variety of reasons, the magnificent ice fields had shrunk by 26 percent since 2000, and Sunday agreed, saying he hadn't seen snow at Shira in the last fifteen years. In fact, we had to climb from Shira at 13,000 feet all the way to 15,000 feet before we finally arrived at the base of one of the ice fields.

The day's climb was scheduled to take approximately seven hours, which, along with our lunch break, would bring us to camp at around 5:30—well before sunset. We began by crossing the Bastain Stream, where the trail became a constant upslope, which progressively got steeper as we approached Lava Tower, the highest point of that day's climb. Between the increase in altitude and the constant uphill climb, our breathing became significantly more labored. Lava Tower is at the base of Kibo and, with an elevation of 15,100 feet, is a perfect detour for getting acclimated to the higher altitudes.

Ryan was the first to show serious signs of altitude sickness, with a pounding headache and dizziness. Emmanuel noticed it as we reached the tower and immediately escorted him to the bottom, while keeping him hydrated.

Our climb to the tower was at a slightly slower pace than was anticipated. We were assured that the remainder of the climb would take about two and a half hours. Julie's knee was still bothering her, but we felt that the pace was pretty good, given the time left to reach Barranco Camp. As the recipient of multiple knee surgeries, including two total knee replacements, I have extensive experience with knee pain and am fully aware that it is much more painful climbing down than climbing up. The remainder of this climb was downhill over boulders with no discernible trail. It was going to be difficult, slow, and painful.

After we climbed for another four hours on what was supposed to be a "two-and-a-half-hour journey," the sun was beginning to set and we could see no campground. Soon, we began asking the guides how much farther we needed to go. Each replied similarly in various ways, "Don't worry, everything is going well." For some reason, that didn't seem right. A short time later, darkness fell. We put on our headlamps and literally stumbled down the steep canyon trails. I was grateful for my steel-toed and waterproof boots, which helped provide stability, while keeping my feet warm and dry.

During the climb, I was getting angry with the non-responses from our guides, because they would not provide any actual information regarding the amount of time required to reach camp. Finally, after ten hours, we saw the lights of Barranco Camp. By then, we were in total darkness, exhausted and ill tempered. Three of us went to sign in, as each camp requires, while Ryan and Julie went directly to their tents. Both of them were suffering from altitude sickness, and Julie needed to give her knees a rest.

Signing in requires your name, date of birth, address, profession, names of guides, and permit number. The guides sign in first, which

Stopping to acclimate at Lava Tower

Descending rocks after Lava Tower

allows the other to simply put "ditto" marks beneath the last three columns. After Philemon, Justin signed in for himself and Julie in an incredibly short time, and I went next. Then I noticed Justin had put "ditto" marks under every category. I asked whether he was suffering from altitude sickness or was simply an idiot. He chose the latter.

Ryan and Julie were both able to join us for dinner. Everyone was being quiet after all the frustration and anger about the day's events. As I tend to do, I waited with my response, while I collected my thoughts. Jill, however, decided it was the perfect time to confront Philemon and the other guides about not answering our questions about our progress and estimated arrival.

Things became heated, as we instructed Philemon from that point forward to answer fully and honestly any questions we asked. We understood his desire to protect us from bad news, but that approach to bad news didn't work for us. We could deal with anything, if given the facts. In addition, we were worried about the summit climb, which was two nights away. If it took us ten hours to make a six-hour climb, how long would it take us to summit? We were told the summit could take anywhere from six to eighteen hours, depending on each individual.

I had been wondering if Julie would be able to make the summit. That evening, Julie mentioned that her knee was beginning to feel a little better. Her determination was inspiring. I was also concerned about Ryan's severe headache and dizziness. What if his symptoms became more acute? His oxygen concentration was horrible that night. Hopefully, he would recover in time. Those concerns, combined with the frustration of the day, were on my mind as we headed for some well-deserved sleep. That night, we all decided to take our Diamox before retiring, even though, in my case, there were no symptoms. I attributed this to my use of the hypoxic tent. Diamox is a prescription diuretic that is often used to treat glaucoma and epilepsy, but is very helpful in reducing the risk of mountain sickness, specifically the complications of hydrocephalus, the buildup of fluid within the brain. Just like the night before, it was freezing. I added hand and feet warmers to my sleeping attire.

JULIE

Shira Camp rests at an elevation of 13,000 feet. To reach Uhuru Peak on Kibo Summit, we had to climb about 7,000 feet higher. Even though that is less than one and a half miles, it takes quite an amount

Carefully descending rocks after Lava Tower

of time and effort to hike uphill. Success at summiting depends on many factors; climbing too quickly, or improperly, leads to adverse health effects. Climbing too fast leads to altitude sickness, which can resemble the flu or a hangover. If left untreated or unmonitored, it can progress into something potentially fatal and requiring immediate attention. The only "cure" is to descend—and fast.

This is why Vern selected a seven-day, six-night ascent of the mountain. Some groups ascend at a faster pace, but their summit success rate isn't as high as the rate for groups doing longer climbs.

The climb from Shira to Barranco Camp heads up a ridge in a direct line toward Uhuru. After we made it to the top of one ridge, another would pop up behind it, as if in an endless succession. The vistas were amazing. The route traversed a semi-desert, and in every direction lay giant chunks of rock that Kibo had expelled during one of her eruptions. Because of our pace the day before, our guides assumed we'd continue hiking at the same slow rate. They even had the porter crew set up our lunch tent about three to four hours away from Shira Camp to feed us hot soup, hot tea, a warm main dish, fruit, and assorted random "appetizers" (which, with every step forward, were becoming increasingly less appetizing). In retrospect, the lunch break was a bad idea. Due to my injury, our pace was already slow. Taking an hour-long lunch break was too much of a delay.

After lunch, we headed toward the Lava Tower—a large rock formation that juts out vertically along the mostly flat land. The base of the Lava Tower is at approximately 15,000 feet, so our guides had us sit for a few minutes to acclimate to the height before hiking down to Barranco Camp, which, at 13,000 feet, is just 500 feet higher than Shira Camp.

Although we would actually be sleeping at nearly the same elevation as the night before, the trek up to the Lava Tower is an important one, because it exposes climbers to a higher elevation for a short period of time. Because I was lost in my own little world of pain, I was unaware that Ryan was not feeling well. Luckily, Emmanuel was there to help him.

The entire time after Lava Tower we walked on and on, thinking camp would be around the next corner. When the guides refused to honestly answer our questions about how much longer we would be hiking, it angered us.

At one point, as my pain grew, I said to Justin, "I don't care how far we are from camp, I just want to know how long it's going to take. Are we two more hours away? More? Less? I need to know. Otherwise, I'm going to lose my mind!"

Justin point-blank asked our head guide how far we had to go. His question was ignored. Feeling a flash of anger, I turned to another guide and asked, "How long until camp?"

"Not long. *Hakuna matata*," he said.

"So you won't give us a time?" A wave of blood went to my temples, and my face became flush with frustration.

There was a sharp falloff next to the trail that was difficult to navigate in the light. Traversing it in the dark with only headlamps, as we later had to do, was particularly dangerous—especially with my bad knee. By this time, all of us were frustrated—pissed off, to be honest. When in that mood, I cry. Justin, who was behind me on the trail, said he could see my tears splashing down on the trail in front of him.

Enjoying breakfast in the sun

Waiting to take on the Barranco Wall

Crossing a brook

It took another hour and a half to reach camp. We had been hiking for over ten hours. Other climbers had been in camp for several hours, relaxing and gearing up for the next day's climb up the Barranco Wall and to Karanga Camp. Our group was tired, cold, hurt, sick, and beyond frustrated. In addition, Ryan's health had taken a downturn, with a severe headache and some nausea.

Since the beginning of the climb, after both breakfast and dinner, our guides tested our pulse rates and blood oxygen levels with an oximeter—a device that measures the percentage of blood loaded with oxygen. The lower the number, the worse it is. At sea level, a normal reading is in the high 90s, and it decreases as climbers ascend. For the last couple of days, our collective group percentages were from the upper 70s to just over 90. I tested surprisingly in the 80s, despite a persistent headache that wrapped around the front of my head with intense pressure. The nausea made it nearly impossible to eat or drink. Vern, Justin, and Jill also tested within the normal range. We would find out Ryan's numbers in the morning.

JUSTIN

Today's climb to Barranco Camp was less scenic than the two days prior. The path weaved its way through desert and boulders.

In spite of our slow climb the day before, our guides insisted we sit in tents after lunch. Because our guides were highly trained experts, we figured they knew what they were doing.

Then came our frustration with our guides for not fessing up about how much time it would take to get to Barranco Camp. Why wouldn't

Philemon, Sunday, and Emmanuel give us an estimated time? Julie and I figured if I asked Philemon directly, he would give us the answer. But he wouldn't, and his body language and overall demeanor ticked me off.

By the time we arrived in Barranco Camp, it was pitch dark, and we were well past the six hours allotted for the hike.

Walking up to our camp, I noticed ice crystals were forming on our tent. It looked like another difficult night, trying to stay warm.

JILL

Each night, my goal was to make it until morning without needing to get up to use Tent #1. Unfortunately, at 2:00 a.m., I had to venture into the freezing cold and take care of business. Swearing out loud with every move I made (as if that was going to make things warmer), I slowly got out of my sleeping bag and stepped outside. The sky was so clear, I could see thousands of stars in the sky and the moonlight reflecting off Kibo's glacier. I could swear there was more visible detail of the mountain by moonlight than at daybreak.

I climbed back into the tent and hoped for some good sleep. The next thing I knew, I heard the soft beating of drums in the distance, followed by a sweet riff on the synthesizer, as the music of Toto let me know it was the next day and soon Kennedy would be at my tent door. On this day, the sun was shining, as we ate our breakfast outside the walls of the mess hall. When I looked around, it seemed like every third porter was on his cell phone. It was great to see Julie in good spirits, as the guides tested her strength and ability to move by making her do several

Ryan and Jill strike a pose, waiting to climb Barranco Wall

Taking a rest

squats in a row without pain. She passed the test with little evidence of discomfort (or any she let on). We left behind Shira Camp as we hiked along the trail, anxious to see what Day 3 had in store.

Philemon, our main guide, led us along a rock path lined with cairns and past one of Mt. Kilimanjaro's indigenous plants, called the *Lobelia Deckennii*. This arid plant doesn't flower until it has been alive for eight years. The one we saw stood three feet tall and looked a lot like a cactus version of Mr. Potato Head when Philemon placed my baseball hat and sun-glasses on it. As the trail progressed, the vegetation began to get sparser, and then, farther up the trail, there was none. The trail snaked in and out of enormous porous black boulders, giving proof that the volcano we were about to climb once had been active. The dark volcanic rocks were spattered with bright orange lichen that shone brightly in contrast to the black boulders.

We walked in and out of rocks larger than four cars piled on top of each other. Some of the rock looked whittled away by an artist with a dark abstract vision.

After lunch, we set out for the Lava Tower. That was when Ryan started to complain about having an intense headache. It proved to be something that would not go away, even when he tried hydrating himself. As we reached our destination, the plan was to acclimate for up to fifteen minutes before continuing on to Barranco Camp, which was at a lower elevation. This was when Emmanuel took Ryan down from the Lava Tower to a lower elevation. As we got closer to Barranco, we saw Ryan and Emmanuel waiting for us along the trail. By this time, he was feeling better. With our group back together, we set out for our long, frustrating walk to camp.

Ryan maneuvering through a crevice

Approaching the base of Kibo

Though we were all tired, the path through the Barranco Valley treated us with the lushest vegetation of the day, as we walked along a deep river bed with a sparse amount of water. Scattered along the valley floor were *Lobelia* trees, which stood tall along the river.

But as it got dark and we couldn't even see our camp, I was beginning to feel uneasy about how the day was going to end. In addition, the temperature was beginning to drop. With each step, I became angrier. For the next forty-five minutes, prior to our arrival, we had to rely on our headlamps. I was frustrated, tired, hungry, out of water, and a headache had started to kick in.

Finally, we saw lights in the distance. Were we getting close to camp? While still farther away than I would have hoped, it provided visual proof that the day was about to end.

RYAN

Due to the increase in elevation, along with the fact that Julie's knee wasn't getting any better, this was without a doubt the toughest day to date.

When we left Shira Camp, the elevation was just above 13,000 feet. As we neared the Lava Tower (15,100 feet), I could tell my pace had slowed, and a severe headache began to set in—not to mention random dizzy spells. At this point, none of the group had taken any high attitude meds (specifically, Diamox). We were hoping to make the summit without the need of medication, but after we reached the Lava Tower, I realized this would change.

Instead of acclimating at the tower for fifteen minutes as required, I opted to continue downward to the next camp. I couldn't bear the thought of spending any more time at that elevation, because I needed to relieve some of the head pressure. At that point, I seriously considered taking some Diamox. Emmanuel and I then made our descent and eventually arrived at that night's camp, with an elevation of about 13,000 feet. It was crazy how one could immediately feel the impact of the higher elevations and how the pressure subsided immediately upon descent.

At camp that night, I was unable to eat and still had a bit of a headache. For some odd reason, the guides didn't want me to take any medication (not sure why, but they wanted us to make the summit without the use of meds). Just before bed, I decided, along with the others, that it was time to pop some pills and avoid a repeat of our experience that day. Fortunately, I was able to fall asleep fairly quickly. Once I woke up, I felt like a different person. Blood oxygen levels were back to normal, and I was ready to take on the Barranco Wall. Thank god for Diamox.

Next: Barranco Camp (13,000 ft.) to Karanga Camp (13,100 ft.).
Distance: 3.1 miles, 4 to 5 hours.

Day 4 Friday, August 8.

VERN

Crawling out of my tent that morning, I looked around to see the scenery we'd missed the night before. To our right, across the canyon floor, was an enormous rock face known as the Barranco Wall. This would be our first severe climbing challenge as we ascended that perpendicular wall. Miraculously, Ryan had a complete transformation overnight, and his oxygen reading was back to normal. What a relief. Both his and Jill's headaches had also diminished. With new understanding between us and our guides, we were ready to take on that damn wall!

As we began the climb, Ryan decided to show us the waterproof quality of his boots and gaiters, so he plunged up to his knee in the small stream the rest of us chose to step over. While many groups might express empathy for such unfortunate mishaps, actions like these provide hours of entertainment at the expense of the victim.

It seemed everyone at the camp had decided to climb the wall at exactly the same time, causing a serious traffic jam at its base. While we ascended, each hand placement was critical. As we crawled, pulled, and jumped from rock to rock, each climber followed the same two-foot-wide trail. The porters, however, were literally climbing nearly straight up the wall—even though there was a drop of hundreds of feet awaiting a misstep. About an hour into our ascent, one of the porters climbing directly above us lost his footing and tumbled

Vern enjoying the climb

Decked out lobelia deckenii plant

Beginning climb toward Kissing Rock on Barranco Wall

down into Jill. Fortunately for both of them, Jill was stable enough to withstand the impact—saving both from a disastrous, and possibly fatal, fall. The porters do not get paid nearly enough. And without them, there is no way to make the climb.

Emmanuel kept talking about Kissing Rock, and how we were going to love it. While the name might bring visions of two lovers overlooking a beautiful valley, the reality is much different. It is called Kissing Rock because the only way to get past it is to get your face as close as possible, find a spot to grip the rock on each side, and slide your feet around the rock, as your heels hang over an immediate drop off. A very invigorating experience, and a rock I will remember forever.

Reaching the top of the canyon is unbelievably exhilarating and all climbers celebrate with pictures of themselves overlooking the canyon, while also looking up, as it is a breathtaking opportunity to view Uhuru over the awe-inspiring glaciers.

Emmanuel informed me that from this point, the trail would be much easier until we began to summit—mostly consisting of a lot of small hills and valleys. Luckily, Julie's knee appeared to be slightly better, even though her ability to flex was severely limited. Our pace was much better, and one large valley stood between us and a good night's rest. From our vantage point, we could see Karanga Camp across the deep valley. While it seemed close, by now we knew better and that it was still hours away. On the path, the shale creates a slippery surface, and each step stirs up a cloud of dust. Climbing up the shale proved to be a different challenge, with one step forward followed by a half step slide back. The steep downward climb was even more difficult, with the combination of gravity and slippery rocks that caused each of us to fall at least once. At one point Justin fell, picked himself up, and fell a second time before he could take another step.

While the food we were being served was significantly better than that at many of the other camps, it was still pretty bland. Our meals started with hot tea and soup, followed by a rather plain, yet generous main course with hot sauce for seasoning.

At dinner, Jill and Julie both expressed concern about some constipation they had been experiencing—a common side effect of high altitude. The guides knew the perfect answer—ginger tea—which was featured along with some ginger in the meal. As always, we were encouraged to hydrate, hydrate, hydrate.

Vern waiting his turn to climb the Barranco Wall

Unlike the last two days, our pace that day was good. Julie's knee seemed to be holding up, Ryan had overcome his altitude sickness (as demonstrated by his return to bragging about his beloved Seahawks), the ginger tea had worked its magic, and Justin and I kept plodding along. We felt ready to take on the challenge ahead. The only unknown was the effect the altitude might have on us. Marathon runners, bike racers, and even professional athletes, like Martina Navratilova and Ray Rice, have tried but were prevented from reaching Uhuru, due to their bodies' inability to adjust to the lack of air pressure. We would soon find out if we were up to the challenge.

The accelerated pace allowed us to have a more relaxing meal, and, after our briefing, we enjoyed a few games of Yahtzee. This was when I shared a concern I had regarding the amount of cash it would require to tip our porters and guides. My luggage had a significant amount of cash, but because the guide company told us we would have twelve porters and two guides, I did not plan for the numbers actually assigned, which turned out to be twenty porters, a cook, and three guides. We discussed the amount we would tip the porters, with a little extra for the cook, much more money for the guides than suggested, and an extra tip for Kennedy—whom we'd interacted with frequently as he served us our meals, cleared our table, magically found another bottle of hot sauce, and awoke us every morning with a scratch on our tents, accompanied by a huge smile while bringing us our tea and water. We all agreed an extra tip was warranted for him.

Believing we were now settled on the tip distribution, Justin blurted out, "What about Duncan?"

We all looked at him in disbelief, and one of us asked, "Who's Duncan?

Preparing to scale a large boulder on the Barranco Wall

A distant view of the previous evening's camp

"You know, the guy who serves us tea in the morning and dinner at night!"

"Do you mean Kennedy?" we asked incredulously.

Justin had no idea where the name Duncan came from, as he didn't even know anyone with that name. Extreme altitude does strange things to your mind.

JULIE

I don't recall much about my quality of sleep at Barranco Camp. I fell asleep pretty fast and, for the first time, did not require getting up in the middle of the night. Now, all I needed was for my headache and nausea to go away.

As dawn broke over camp and the sunlight gradually appeared, I opened my eyes to a clear head. No headache and no pressure. My knee was still in pain, but I could deal with it. Exiting our tent, I looked to my left, and there was Kibo looming large over our camp. It was spectacular.

This was the morning we were to conquer the Barranco Wall, a nearly 900-foot wall with a steep incline that boasts a mostly single-file trail slicing upward, over and through jagged rocks, perching climbers precariously close to the vertigo-inducing ledge. From our viewpoint, it looked insane.

As we left camp, we could see a colorful trail of climbers and porters carefully making their way up the wall. Though there appeared to be just one well-trodden path stomped down between the rocks, we could see porters, with their fifty pounds of baggage, sure-footedly scampering above and below the packed climber trail. The porters

Julie demonstrating the "kiss" at the famous Kissing Rock

were finding shortcuts where no sane people would dare set foot. Once again, their graceful agility astounded us.

I looked up and contemplated our climb. It was not technical, meaning no ropes or other climbing equipment was necessary to reach the top of the ridge. However, I could see how my trekking poles would quickly become a liability. A couple of evenings prior, our porters had told us about Kissing Rock, which is near the midway point. Kissing Rock sits on a very narrow ledge. To cross it, climbers need to turn and face the rock, while shuffling their feet side to side and hugging the rock wall, hoping for good handholds.

After we waited a good half hour for people to pass, it was finally our turn. Up and over we went. At one point, we came to a drop-off that was just over waist high. I made my way safely down, and then turned after hearing a commotion behind me. Spinning around, I saw a girl fly off the ledge I had so carefully descended. She bumped into the back of Jill, who thankfully slowed her down. Without Jill as a speed bump, I'm certain she would have tumbled over the edge. Strangely, she was laughing her ass off. I shook my head, rolled my eyes, and turned back around—more grim and focused than before.

As we neared Kissing Rock, I was a bit underwhelmed. It wasn't what I was expecting. It looked like every other rock on the trail, except that the trail was a bit narrower. I turned to face the rock and slowly took a cautious step with my right foot. Looking down over my right shoulder, my terra firma disintegrated into loose rock and dust on a downward slope to the ground—far, far below. Looks were definitely deceiving. I took a shuffle step with my left foot, and then again with my right. My arms and hands, stretching to my fullest wingspan,

Reaching halfway point to the top of Barranco Wall

hugged the rock, as my fingers searched for a decent nook or cranny to grab. Shuffle step again.

"Julie!" our guide Sunday called out. He was taking photographs, leaping over and below us with ease, snapping shots of us all. I was instructed to kiss the rock, which I did. In fact, I kissed it for a very long time. So long, people had to nudge me out of my puckered fear to get me moving. After several more shuffle steps and adjusted handholds, I was finally beyond it.

Once over Barranco Wall, we were rewarded with a spectacular view of Uhuru. After a brief snack break and rest, we began to move toward Karanga Camp. Our total climbing time that day was supposed to be four to six hours, an "easy" climb that allows climbers to rest a bit prior to the big summit push.

Hand placement by Emmanuel is crucial

Jill and Ryan ascending Barranco

From a high ridge, we could finally see the colorful tents at camp. They didn't look very far away, but we had smartened up a bit to realize that in mountain-time, we were still about an hour and a half away.

That night, food didn't interest me, nor did water. Progressively, each camp was colder, forcing me to add more clothes before bed. I also began placing hand warmers between my sock base layers and into my gloves, in the hope of getting a good night's sleep.

The next morning, we were departing for Barafu Camp, which, at 15,300 feet, is summit base camp. Though we moved at a much faster speed this day, the amount of quality rest prior to the summit push was dependent on a timely arrival at Barafu Camp. My knee still hurt quite a bit, but by this point I had learned how to maneuver my way around any movements that prevented me from simply moving forward. I was feeling positive, but exhausted.

JUSTIN

I was glad the previous day was over and looked forward to our climb up the Barranco Wall. As we climbed the rocks and pulled ourselves over boulders, everyone in our group smiled. We were finally on the same page with our guides.

Watching Julie's experience with Kissing Rock was interesting. As she approached the rock, she stopped and looked back toward us. Nonverbally, we tried telling her not to think about anything—especially the hundred-yard drop if she lost her footing. The idea was to reach around the rock, press your chest against it, and slide your leg around to the other side. Then, in no time, it would be over. Instead, Julie made her first move and then reached as far as she could to the other side of the rock, while placing her chest against the rock. At that point, she stalled until Emmanuel grabbed her arm and helped her get past the rock. Then, one by one, our group followed, with everyone kissing the rock.

After that, we had to jump off a small four-foot-high cliff. Though it doesn't sound like much, the landing spot was only six feet deep. An accidental stumble would have resulted in a 120-foot fall straight down to the rocks below.

After making it to the top of the wall, we stopped to take a group picture of us looking over the wall, with nothing behind us but clouds. Earlier, we were told that the climb up the wall would be the most challenging part of the day. From there, we would be hiking through gentle hills and valleys. It was our first introduction to shale, which consists of flat rocks with a slippery surface that can easily put you on your backside. While I was able to keep my footing at first, Julie wasn't as lucky, and at one point she lost her footing and fell to the ground. After mocking her, I ended up falling. Not once but twice—which delighted both Julie and Vern.

JILL

We awoke to the ground covered with frost, which soon began to melt as we ate our breakfast. I was relieved that Ryan had made a dramatic comeback after getting some rest. The camp was filled with large groups of people from all over the world, with many climbing for causes and proudly wearing matching T-shirts. As I sipped on my coffee, looking at the wall ahead of us, I could faintly see the brightly colored line of people as they made their way straight up the wall.

Celebrating Day 4 on the Wall

Jill scooting down a boulder on the Barranco Wall

As happened most days, we were one of the last groups to leave camp. On Day 3, the porters seemed to be working faster and had even more hustle than the other days. We were told that the porters on this day would have the right of way, due to the challenge of climbing the Barranco Wall. As we approached the wall, it was becoming very clear that this was a different level of climbing than previous days.

Before getting to the wall, we crossed a small riverbed. Ryan had managed to find what seemed to be the one puddle in all of Barranco Camp, resulting in him sinking so deep in mud, it almost covered the height of his gator.

We didn't get very far up the side of the wall before finding a safe place for us all to sit, as the long line of porters walked by. Those hard-working men often appeared to defy gravity, as each one scurried up the walls using only one hand, with the other clinging to a bag balancing on his shoulders and neck. The porters often lost their patience as they tried to avoid the lines that formed, oftentimes making their own trail without showing any fear of possibly falling over a cliff.

When our time finally came, Julie led the pack, and I followed closely behind. Our guides helped us maneuver our way safely, offering a helping hand or instructing us with precise instructions on where to place our feet and hands to get us up the side of the rock face without slipping.

Once we reached the top of the wall, there was a breathtaking view over the valley and the mountains below. Chills ran down my spine, as I looked at how many vertical feet we had scrambled up to be where we were standing. We took a short break, knowing we had a way to go before reaching camp.

Philemon and Justin making their way up the Barranco Wall

Jill and Ryan jumping atop the Barranco Wall

The trail we traveled on was long and very dusty with the vegetation becoming more sparse, probably because precipitation was so rare. In fact, we reached a point where we could see camp, but realized that seeing camp didn't mean it was close. The trail was very hilly as we made our way to the bottom of the valley. Much of the trail was composed of loose shale, which did not make for good traction. Everyone in our group took turns losing footing and either sticking the landing or sometimes landing safely on their butts. As we neared camp, there was another large hill to conquer with a little bit of bouldering left, but it seemed like nothing compared to what we had done on the Barranco Wall.

We walked into camp with higher spirits than we had the previous day, all of us covered in dust.

RYAN

After my bout with altitude sickness, the next morning I felt like a new man. This was the day I was to experience my favorite part of the climb (besides the summit, of course), the Barranco Wall. The wall is a nearly 900-foot face that requires climbers to boulder up in some sections. This means we had to use our hands to climb from rock to rock. It isn't a technical climb, which would require a harness, but is nevertheless extremely steep and exposed. Anyone taking one or two steps in the wrong direction could face dire consequences. That's how open the face of the wall is.

Next: Karanga Camp (13,100 ft.) to Barafu (Summit Base) Camp (15,3000 ft.).

Day 5: Saturday, August 9

VERN

As usual, at sunrise I was served hot tea by a smiling Kennedy. A minute later I heard Justin's voice greeting him with a bubbly, "Good morning, Duncan," followed by a quick, "Damn it, I did it again!"

It was nice to start the day with a good laugh.

Ready for Day 5

Justin and I learned a very valuable lesson regarding the ginger we had consumed in various forms the night before, which allowed the girls to relieve their constipation. As it turns out, that much ginger consumption for those without constipation results in several hours of making frequent trips for relief, beginning in the middle of the night. I still avoid ginger to this day.

The trail this day made me think of the landscape of the moon, with large boulders scattered among slippery, dust-covered rocks—the result of volcanic eruptions. For the first time in days, there were many places where the trail widened to a point where climbers could maneuver two or three abreast. This allowed us to pass and be passed by other climbers. Oddly, we seldom interacted with others, due to language differences, other than to provide the polite reminder, *pole-pole*. But on this day we were pleasantly surprised when we passed

Justin and Julie on Day 4

a group of climbers who were American. For a time, as the width of the trail allowed, we matched their pace and had one of our first opportunities to engage in conversation with someone outside our group. Unfortunately, two of the women in the group were engaged in an animated conversation about a television show they believed was the dumbest show ever—*Family Guy*, which just happened to be a show we all enjoyed. This led Justin and Ryan to carry on their own conversation about how funny they thought the show was. Each group alternated to increase the volume of the conversation to prove their point without actually speaking to the other. These competing passive-aggressive conversations cut short our opportunity to learn more about the members of that group. I'm not sure that we can attribute this behavior solely to the altitude.

We arrived at Barafu Camp at 12:30, which was about an hour ahead of schedule. Awesome news because two nights earlier, after the brutal climb to Barranco Camp, Philemon and Sunday estimated our climb to the summit would require at least ten hours. Sunday was now convinced we could summit in six to seven hours, in time to watch the sun rise.

After lunch, we were instructed to take a nap, as we would be climbing during the entire night. For me, it was impossible. In front of us was an incredible view of the trail we would take to Uhuru. To our east, we had a beautiful view of Mawenzi Peak, the second highest peak on Mt. Kilimanjaro—a peak featuring jagged rock spires, culminating in a cathedral-like summit, making it so unstable that it is rarely climbed. After I'd dreamed about being in the place for all those years and with my goal directly in front of me, sleep was impossible.

We had a most unusual campsite, with virtually no flat spots or space between huge boulders. Climbing the boulders to the mess tent was a challenge, and even Tent #1 required navigating the uneven rocks.

Amazingly, I was again able to reach Irene via phone, though the connection was a bit difficult. I really needed to speak with her one last time before our final ascent. As always, she wanted to know how our health, both physical and mental, was holding up. She rarely asked about my knees, which, I assumed, was to avoid having me think about how fortunate I was that my twenty-year-old artificial joints were carrying me so well.

After the phone call and still unable to sleep, I found a couple of boulders to sit on and settled in to finish *Cosmos*, one of the books I'd brought. After a few minutes, I felt a tugging on my back pocket.

Julie takes a tumble

Julie leading the way down into Karanga Valley

It turned out to be a chipmunk, nearly identical to those we have in Michigan, tugging at an empty peanut bag in my pocket. For the next few minutes, the two of us shared a bag of nuts. Two uplifting connections to home, here in deep Africa.

JULIE

Our initial hike on Day 5 proved to be a rather short one. After packing up at Karanga Camp, we headed toward Barafu Summit Base Camp—which stands at 15,300 feet. On our way up, we passed the junction that connects with the Mweka trail, which is the route we would be taking the next day on the way down the mountain.

I had not tweaked my knee in almost two days, and while it still hurt badly, I was feeling more positive about actually making it to the top for the first time in the last few days. But now I had a more pressing issue, one that was enormously frustrating: my stomach was in complete upheaval. Before hitting the trail toward Barafu, I had to hit Tent #1 with some urgency. This was not good. Just a couple of evenings ago, we (the women) were experiencing the complete opposite symptoms and had asked for a remedy for a sluggish digestive tract. The cure was piping hot ginger tea, which worked for all of us, to varying degrees (and definitions).

Typically, the campsites are the only flat surfaces we encounter during the day. Barafu Camp was the exception, with our tents wedged between huge boulders, and getting to our meal tent, or Tent #1, required careful foot placement as we scaled the rocky incline.

Ryan, Jill, and Vern on Day 4

Happy to be at camp in time for the actual lunch hour, our group was in good spirits. This was a good thing, because we had an endless day ahead of us. The panoramic view from Barafu was incredible. In the last several days, we had completed the South Circuit of Mt. Kilimanjaro, which presented us with many different views of the mountain. From Barafu Camp, we could see the third peak, Mawenzi, in the distance, standing at a very spiky 16,893 feet.

We were instructed to rest, but it was the middle of the day, the sun was shining bright, and we were surrounded by porters who would not be making that night's climb with us. So, while we were supposed to be resting and sleeping, they were chatting and laughing it up. Apparently, they had given no thought to our mandatory quiet time. Thankfully, Jill had brought ear plugs (she thought of everything), and I used them to mute the conversation. I don't think Justin slept at all, though.

A few hours later we were called to dinner. By this time, my stomach was rolling, and I had horrible gastrointestinal pain. I could not eat or drink, partly because the altitude had killed my appetite (which is normal) and partly because I was afraid anything I ingested would go right through me during the worst moment possible. I asked Vern if he had any medication, and he rifled through his medical kit for an anti-diarrheal. He brought it with him to dinner, and we asked our guides if they "approved" of it for me. Because it was not a name brand, they were hesitant about me taking it, and began asking around other groups to see if they had Imodium. I was miserable. I was cold, my stomach hurt, my knee hurt, the food turned my stomach, and I could not drink the three liters of water that was recommended.

Dinner at Karanga Camp

Awesome scene of Uhuru from Karanga Camp

Our guide Philemon assists Julie on the last stretch up to Uhuru Peak

As I sat staring at my untouched plate of food, one of the guides finally handed me a four-pack of Imodium and instructed that I take one. I was not very familiar with the dosage and asked when I could take the next pill (we were about five hours away from taking our first steps toward the summit). The answer to that question changed a few times, ranging from "Three hours" to "Let's just wait and see." Um—wait and see? Wait and see if I had an accident going up the mountain? Though I wanted to, and others did on my behalf, I didn't argue with him. I did not want things to swing wildly in the other direction.

After dinner and tea, we retreated once again into our tents at around 8 p.m. I had not eaten more than one bite of food since breakfast and had not drunk any significant amounts of water for several hours. I was out of fuel, dehydrated, exhausted, and my stomach was rolling and gurgling around. On top of that, my knee still hurt. I kept telling myself "One more climb, and we'll be there!" and "By this time tomorrow, we'll have made it!" and "I made it this far, I can make it one more day!" The positive mantras would evolve into more profanity-laced ones early the next day, but those mantras helped me up the mountain.

After putting on all the articles of clothing that I was going to be summiting in (some twenty items—I counted), I lay down in my sleeping bag to try and rest. Nope. That was not going to work. I had some of Justin's summit clothes stuffed into the end of my sleeping bag to keep them warm (they would not fit in his), and I was legitimately worried about having an accident on them.

I will spare the details, but what happened next was not good. It will be a long time before I forget my mom's hysterical laughter when I told her the story later on. Long story short, I put my headlamp on my head and hauled myself out of my tent and into the frigid air toward Tent #1. Two things I will mention about this once-in-a-lifetime experience: (1) Tent #1 was the single most important and fabulous piece of equipment we had, and (2) Despite the "luxury," as I explained to my mom, "It offered us visual privacy—though not audible." Which is all I need to say about my experience that night.

Feeling much better thirty minutes later, I climbed back into my sleeping bag and managed to get a couple of hours of sleep. We would be getting a wake-up call at 11 p.m. to get ready for a midnight start up the mountain.

JUSTIN

As always, at sunrise, I was greeted by a smiling Kennedy and my hot tea. Once again I called him "Duncan." By now, he was used to it, so we all had a good laugh.

On Day 5, the sun was out again, and temps were in the 50s. We were surrounded by incredible views. Looking in one direction, we could see our destination, the summit. In the opposite direction, we saw the clouds below. Seeing the clouds will remain a great memory, reminding us of how high we had already climbed.

After we arrived at Barafu Camp around 12:30, the guides gave us a little time to hang out before being forced to drink tea or slurp soup. Looking around, (and after signing Julie and myself into camp), I was amazed that Barafu was considered a camp. Because it was built on the side of the mountain, we had to climb boulders to get to our tent. And because of the blowing wind, to keep our

Eruption debris

tents in place, they were positioned on top of boulders and held down with smaller rocks.

Dinner was early, at around 4:30, because we needed to start our summit assault at midnight. I was both excited and anxious. So much so, I lost my appetite. Knowing I had to eat something, I forced myself to eat.

Soon, it was off to bed.

RYAN

On Day 5, we climbed to Barafu Base Camp, which is at 15,239 feet. My only fear was that I was climbing above 15,000 feet again and wasn't sure how my body would react the second time around. Fortunately, I

Vern, Jill, and Ryan holding up a boulder

had been taking Diamox for over a day now, and the medication was well into my bloodstream. I convinced myself that all would be well.

As we hiked toward base camp, the terrain reminded me of photos I'd seen of the moon's surface, with long, flat sections dotted with boulders of various sizes. The climb at this section wasn't too difficult. I thought of it as the calm before the storm, since we were just about to reach base camp, and from there, everything was all about the summit push.

To my relief, I didn't feel any effects of the altitude while climbing just to and above the 15,000-foot mark. I guess the Diamox was working. Our plan at base camp was to get to bed early after eating dinner around 5 p.m. At 11 p.m., we were awakened in time to get some breakfast before heading out for the midnight summit.

Chapter 5

YOU CAN TOLERATE ANYTHING
For 30 Minutes

Day 6 Summit Push, Sunday, August 10th

VERN

Following our dinner, I was able to nap for an hour before getting up at 11:00 p.m. for our ascent on the summit. After getting dressed in all of my layers, I headed up the rocks to the mess tent for breakfast and final instructions. Our Camelback bladders, typically filled to the three-liter capacity, were only half filled to reduce the weight we would carry. We reminded one another to blow the water back into the bladder to prevent the hose and the mouthpiece from freezing in the bitter cold, which was exacerbated by the strong wind.

Because every step was uphill, the pace for our climb was extremely slow. Barafu Camp spreads out, since it serves as base camp for four of the routes up the mountain, and there are so few level places for the tents. It took what seemed like an hour just to get through the camp.

During our wait, we watched the long line of headlamps snaking up the cutbacks ahead of us. Placing one foot in front of the other was beginning to be a struggle, as was inhaling as deeply as possible. Our guides recruited one of the porters, who had aspirations of becoming a guide, to join us on the final stage of our summit. While we struggled for each breath, the guides continuously sang songs, told jokes, and shouted out the same Swahili phrases they had done previously, all the while waiting for our appropriate response. The songs were inspiring, especially when they inserted our names into the lyrics. I soon realized that our responding had shifted from a fun language-learning experience to a critical test of our mental state, as they looked for signs of acute altitude sickness. Those symptoms include mental confusion, fainting, the inability to walk in a straight line, and lips turning blue or gray. In the severe stages, they become life threatening. If any of us failed to respond, which happened fairly often, as breathing was tough and talking added to the difficulty, a guide quickly came to our side to make sure we were all right.

After about an hour, we witnessed the first climber being taken off the mountain, due to severe mental confusion. Apparently, she couldn't tell the guide her name. The guides were preparing to carry her down by wrapping duct tape around her upper arms and torso, as her arms hung down her sides, while still allowing her elbow to bend into an "L" position. With a guide on each side, they each lifted up on her elbows, allowing them to support, or even carry, her as they made their way back to base camp. From there, they placed her on a metal stretcher with one pneumatic tire directly in the middle, and three of them wheeled and carried her down to an altitude where she could be safely helicoptered off the mountain.

A climber taken off the mountain

The trail was increasingly steep and the footing precarious, as we continued the ascent up the winding and slippery dust-covered shale and rocks. The milder symptoms of altitude sickness include vomiting and diarrhea, which is very common during the final ascent. The climb becomes a little more difficult as the sound of climbers vomiting breaks the near silence (it also makes the rest of us fight the urge to join them). The trail is usually wide enough for only one person, which caused us to witness these reactions first hand.

Every climber uses various mental tricks to keep moving. Our only goal was putting one foot in front of the other. Years ago, while I recovered from total knee surgery, the rehabilitation was terribly painful. My mantra for getting through that pain was simply: "I can tolerate anything for thirty minutes." I used that same phrase numerous times during this entire climb.

Earlier, our guides had informed us we would be stopping every ninety minutes for a short, five-minute rest. We asked that they let us know our progress in thirty-minute intervals. When they announced sixty minutes before our next break, I would tell myself I could do anything until the next thirty-minute announcement. It worked to perfection for me, as each of us did whatever we could to keep moving one foot at a time, one deep breath with every step.

Despite my best efforts to force the water from the mouthpiece tube back into the bladder, my entire water bladder was frozen before our first five-minute break. This meant no more water for the rest of the climb.

Unlike the earlier part of our climb, conversations were now rare. I remember only four brief exchanges during the seven hours it took us to summit.

Shortly before our second five-minute break, we had entered a particularly difficult part of the climb. At one point, after Justin slid backward, barely catching himself, he turned and yelled, "Vern, what the hell did you get us into?" I was beginning to wonder the same thing.

At the second break, Jill had diarrhea and went over to a somewhat secluded area, slightly off the path. Ryan, concerned whether she was all right, went over to check on her. After he focused his headlamp directly on the squatting Jill, we heard, "Get that damn light off me!" I seriously doubt if anyone else even noticed, as all the other climbers were focused on an area one foot ahead, in order to place each foot correctly.

Approaching our third break, I looked up from staring at my feet to survey my surroundings—a rare luxury. In spite of incredible fatigue and lack of sleep and oxygen, I was able to enjoy the beautiful full perigee moon (when the moon is closest to the earth), which is the reason I had chosen August 10 for summiting. How incredible it was to see the magnificent glaciers on each side of us glistening in the brilliant moonlight with millions of radiant stars sparkling in the background.

As these images were seared into my memory, I realized that it was again time to focus all energy back on the climb. Our guide Sunday informed us that another half hour had passed, and I looked above me at what appeared to be an adobe-style building of some sort. My mind had a difficult time processing why I hadn't heard about the building along the summit path, until I realized that I was looking at a rock formation directly above us that was illuminated by climbers' headlamps. That and other hallucinations kept me entertained until I was interrupted by a scream, which again came from Justin: "Vern, I fucking hate you!" To which I could honestly respond, "Yeah, so do I right now."

Finally, after climbing for over six hours, Philemon announced we were thirty minutes to Stella Point, which rests at 18,848 feet and would be the first flat spot we encountered during this grueling climb. This point provided us with an opportunity to sit down for the first time all night. We watched as the guiding, full-moon light began to fade, giving way to the light of dawn.

We had made the climb at an excellent pace and were sitting between two massive glaciers, each rising over one hundred meters above the frozen ground. We could now see the trail to Uhuru, a forty-five-minute climb from where we were. At this point, we all knew we were going to make the summit. Sunday and Emmanuel both began urging us to move on. We were only able to stay at this altitude for a short time

Emmanuel takes a well-deserved break

and needed to quickly get to the peak. I was so excited to get there that I increased my pace and was immediately stopped by Sunday. "*Pole-Pole.*" I hardly needed reminding, because my lungs were giving me a much more forceful message.

This climb was stunning, as we continued being mesmerized by the enormity of the glaciers and the view of the Northern Ice Field—which seemed to stretch for miles. The clouds covered the base of the mountain, much as they had since the first day. However, now we were actually looking at the curvature of the earth, just as the sun rose majestically over the continent of Africa. We were the first people in the entire continent of Africa to see the sun that day.

Very early in the climb, Sunday informed us that the certificates that are issued enter the actual time that each climber reaches Uhuru Peak.

After a few minutes of bragging about who would summit first, we all agreed that we would step to the summit together. We all stepped up to the Uhuru sign at 7:00 a.m., midnight back home, to a series of hugs and kisses. We made it! A guide from another party took a picture of our entire group, after which we were told to descend immediately. The air is so thin that every minute increases the potential of altitude illness, and we were not out of danger yet. My father, one of my heroes, had died the previous November at the age of ninety-one. He was a huge supporter of all my ventures and doubly so for my climbing Kili. In remembrance, I'd brought along one of his favorite lapel pins. I walked a few yards from the sign, removed my mittens, and dug a hole to place the pin. To my surprise, the ash-like ground was warm, in spite of it being sixteen below zero with howling winds. My hand was warm as I dug the hole into the volcanic surface. In exchange, I placed a small rock in my backpack and had a short conversation with Dad. I thanked him for his love, for his life lessons, and for being the most incredible example of living a humble, loving, and compassionate life. Sunday again interrupted me with a more urgent request to begin the descent, immediately.

The kids were already on their way toward Stella Point. Sunday informed me that we were breaking into three groups to descend the mountain down to Barafu Camp. The altitude was clearly affecting me at this point, as my thinking was very dull, much like when I experience a mild concussion. I know what is happening around me, but it takes significantly more time to process everything. I had no idea why we were being separated, but couldn't articulate the question, and simply followed directions. I was assured that we would reunite at Barafu for the remainder of the descent.

As we arrived at the edge of Stella Point, I could finally see the trail we had climbed, while observing those still attempting to summit. Sunday pointed at a guide who was sliding down the mountain and asked, "Do you know how to shale-ski?" I readily admitted that I had never tried it but was willing to learn. Shale-skiing involves going straight down the steepest parts of the shale-covered slope. Using hiking poles for balance, you shove your heel into the shale, which gives way immediately, allowing you to ski on one foot for about eight to ten feet before shoving your other heel into the shale and repeating the sliding action. While you ski in that manner, it is important to be careful to avoid areas where rocks interrupt the loose shale, causing your feet to stop, as the rest of your body continues downward. Shale-skiing definitely gets you down the mountain fast. But it is very dusty, and at 19,000 feet, breathing is still very difficult. The numerous breaks for a much-needed gasp of air allowed me to observe climbers who were being escorted or carried down the mountain, due to either injury or altitude sickness.

I arrived back in Barafu Camp at about 8:45, with Jill and Ryan shortly behind, while Julie and Justin were taking a more deliberate route to accommodate Julie's injured knee. The porters greeted each of us with a special fruit drink to celebrate. They all seemed genuinely happy to see that we had all made it, and I suspect that summiting probably increases the tips they will receive following a successful climb.

As we climbed back to our tents, I mentioned to the kids that I'd thought about calling Irene but wouldn't, because it was the middle of the night back in Michigan, and I didn't want to wake her or the kids. Ryan looked at me and said, "Man, you have to call. You just fucking summited!"

He was right. I called and, between tears from both of us, I said, "We all summited. We made it!" I could hear the relief and joy in Irene's voice, as she was truly invested in this journey and my success. I missed her more at that moment than I could have imagined.

After a short nap and celebratory lunch, we packed for the four-hour climb down to Mweka Camp. During that dusty descent, we again observed climbers being taken down the mountain on stretchers. Descending is actually harder on knee injuries than ascending, and my knees were beginning to ache. So Julie and I kept the same pace.

Since midnight, we had made a brutal ascent and after that climb had descended down to 10,204 feet for our last night on the mountain. I broke out my flask of Laddie Ten Scotch for a well-deserved toast. We each took a sip, savoring the flavor and the resulting relaxation,

Ryan and our guide Philemon

all except for Justin, who thought it was a guzzling contest. Jill and Ryan then brought out their Jack Daniels for a nightcap, which went amazingly well with our after-dinner popcorn.

We also decided to leave very early in the morning, in order to be one of the first groups to sign out and get our certificates, a plan that would get us back to Mt. Meru resort for a long overdue shower.

At that point, we needed to determine the amount of tips to give each person, while dividing the money into manageable piles. We asked Philemon how much a good tip would be for each of the porters. As I feared, we were definitely in trouble in terms of how much cash we had on hand. We had not anticipated the eight additional porters and the one additional guide. And, most important, the guide company we'd hired suggested a tip that was far below the rates suggested by trekking manuals. Finally, I had misplaced some of my money, possibly at Mt. Meru resort. I thought I might have to stop for more cash.

JULIE

After a nervous night's sleep, I opened my eyes in the dark to the sound of Kennedy saying, "Hi-lo. Justin? Julie?" In the words of Rafiki, "It is time! Summit day!"

It was the night of Day 5, at 11 p.m., after we had already hiked four to five hours to the tents we were crawling out of. The same day when we ate lunch, then napped; ate dinner and napped again. The same day when just a couple of hours ago, I was certain that I could not be more than 50 feet away from Tent #1 at all times.

Ryan and Emmanuel heading toward Uhuru Peak,
with Kili's majestic glaciers in the background

Except for the light of the full moon, it was dark. Vern had specifically chosen this full moon to climb under. Though we still needed headlamps to see, it really was an incredible sight. There were no clouds, and we could see stars all across the dome that night.

I had worn pretty much every piece of clothing I'd brought for the climb to bed and had planned on wearing all of them while summiting. They included base layer socks, heavy socks, hiking boots, two pairs of base layer pants, convertible hiking pants, and rain pants over all of them. On my top, I wore a medium and two light upper base layer shirts, one wicking T-shirt, a puffy down vest, and a puffy down jacket, covered by a rain/wind shell. My hands were covered with base layer gloves with mittens over them. Protecting my head and neck were a buff, a balaclava, a hood from my down jacket, and a hood from my rain/wind jacket shell. I walked around like Randy from *A Christmas Story*, saying, "I can't put my arms down!"

I was still feeling some cramping in my stomach, so I headed to the mess tent as a precaution. On previous mornings, for breakfast, our crew had served us porridge sweetened with honey and sugar, which stuck to our ribs. This day, however, someone must have miscalculated the amount of porridge we'd need, resulting in less porridge and more cloudy, scalding water. Gag. Regardless, I could not eat that or anything else, due to my stomach. Instead, I nibbled on a biscuit, which was all I could manage.

We were scheduled to begin our climb at midnight. Prior to our start, I was feeling trepidation that my knee wouldn't hold out. We were heading up to serious altitude, over 19,000 feet, and I had heard many stories about people who couldn't handle the atmosphere at that height. There was also concern about physical exhaustion, because we all had pushed our bodies to the limit all week. To varying degrees, we had battled headaches, knee pain, nausea, loss of appetite, heat, and cold, plus, of course, missing loved ones back home.

I grabbed my trekking poles and looked toward the mountain. Even in the dark, I could see a large glacier that clung onto the side of the mountain shimmering in the moonlight. Other groups of climbers had started out ahead of us, and we could see their headlamps steadily inching their way upward.

The climb to the summit was around 4,000 feet, a distance less than a mile, which could normally be walked in under nine minutes. But because we were going up and over flat and slanted scrapes of rock and through an endless switchback of slippery shale, the climb was scheduled to take anywhere from six to eight hours.

Each step for me had to be carefully managed and strategically placed. If I tweaked my knee now, the remainder of the climb would be more difficult and incredibly painful.

Despite the hundreds of headlamps that threaded their way up the steep slope and disappeared over a ridge, it was still pretty dark. My headlamp revealed just enough ground to keep me safe and moving forward, but did not reveal much of the difficult road ahead. It was like walking with blinders on. What was important was to place one foot in front of the other and just keep moving. That was our only task, and if we strung a bunch of those steps together and did not give up, we would be rewarded with an experience like no other and a well-earned view from the top.

This summit climb was tough. It was frigid, the incline was steep, the ground soft, and our destination completely obscured from view. Even if it had been light out, there was no way to see how much farther we'd have to go. The simplest of efforts had me huffing and struggling to get a full lungful of air into my body. Our guides, who were trained with a good ear for any signs of impending altitude illness, would turn around when they heard my breath rapidly increase, stop me, and say, "Breathe in, all the way in. Then breathe out." Emmanuel would always make me do this three times.

After six hours of climbing, we finally saw dawn breaking to our right and the top of the ridge and Stella Point directly above us. Our

Our first look at Kili's glaciers

guides hustled us past the sign post for Stella Point and past a couple of dozen climbers taking a break. At that point, they nearly ripped off our headlamps and made us take a very short break to refuel and take some pictures. This is where I saw one of the most incredible views ever—Kili's glaciers. They looked nothing like they did from lower altitudes and were not the pure white fluffy caps of snow. From our location, I saw layer upon layer of striated ice. They looked a bit dirty, covered in ash, but they were just magnificent. The sight of them made me physically react. My mouth dropped open, my head recoiled, and I gasped. Again, I believe my enlightened and profound first words were something along the lines of, "Holy shit!"

I could not stop staring at them. However, we still were not at our final destination and needed to get moving. Our guides pointed out the

Kili's grand glaciers

general direction of Uhuru Peak, which was straight ahead, and then took a dogleg right to the very top. Even though we could see it, it was still an hour's climb away.

As we climbed the remaining hills on the way to Uhuru, we had the pleasure of viewing the incredibly scenic caldera that dimpled the top of Kibo Summit. It was much bigger than I had expected. We rounded the final right turn toward Uhuru, and could finally see a colorful crowd of climbers celebrating their achievement. Philemon grabbed the trekking pole out of my left hand and hooked his arm in mine and began helping me forward. I must've been slowing down, or maybe I just looked like I had no fuel left in the tank, because he pretty much dragged me up the last several hundred feet to the signpost.

We had made it to Uhuru Peak! All of us! We all posed for several pictures with the iconic signpost, and laughed and hugged for a few minutes. Then our guides made it clear that it was time to get down—and fast. It was no place to linger.

I was happy to be going down, but quickly remembered that going down sucked worse than going up. We made it back to Stella Point for a photo op, and then began making our way back to Barafu Camp. I don't know if it was the altitude or exhaustion, but I did not realize the challenge that going down would bring. It took seven hours to go up and at least two hours to get down. Our group had split up, with Jill and Ryan going with Philemon and Vern skiing down with Sunday's guidance, followed by Justin and me. It would have required so much more energy for the others to put the brakes on, trying go extra slow on that endless hill.

When we finally got back to camp, we just collapsed in our tents. It felt so good to get our boots off and shed our many layers of clothing. The sun was bright and warm, and we were hot. I don't know the temperature differential between base camp and the summit, but I know I would have been happy descending in shorts, rather than the many articles of clothing required for the summit.

After taking a nap in our sun-warmed tents, we awoke to another prepared meal at base camp and got ready to climb down to Mweka Camp, which stands at 10,024 ft. My body was tired, but I was still feeling a bit of adrenaline from making the summit. We once again packed all of our things and began making our way down.

One of our extra guides for the summit push

JUSTIN

Just like every morning, we were awakened by Kennedy. This time he told us it was summit day!

I asked Julie how she was feeling, and she said slightly better, which was good news. Once we were outside, it was bitter cold. A full moon greeted us and helped light our way to the mess tent. Once again, I was not hungry, but I knew I had to eat something. I put some food in my mouth and just swallowed.

As we began climbing, the guides reminded us, "*Pole, pole.*" Not a problem, my legs were dead and I had no energy. This was the first climb where my legs felt exhausted. I decided to get my mind off the cold and instead focus on how hard it was to catch my breath.

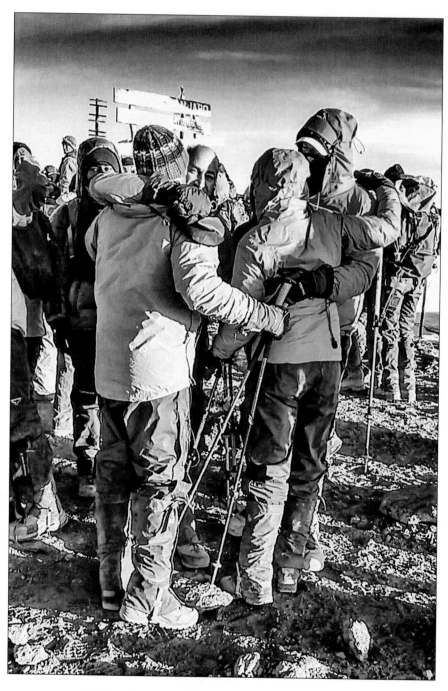

Celebrating upon the Roof of Africa—we did it!

Finally, I got my mind diverted by the incredible stories Julie and I would be able to share with our kids. I began thinking about sharing stories about the trip with my parents. The best part was knowing we would not fail to summit. My fear of failure, or my refusal to fail, was pushing me to the top of Mt. Kilimanjaro to reach Uhuru Peak.

That was around the time I heard Philemon yelling that we had five minutes before our first break. I realized that I had no clue how long we had been climbing. Looking down the mountain, I was able to gauge how far we had climbed and was amazed at our progress. Behind us, I could see a line of lights from other climbers and could no longer see our camp. I had clearly zoned out and lost myself in daydreams.

I did not want to zone out like that again and felt like counting every single step. But soon I was looking ahead of Julie and Philemon, so I could anticipate each turn in front of us. I was also listening to the groups ahead and behind us, hearing deep coughs, gagging, and even the sound of someone puking. The conversations were nothing special, just the normal checks on how others were doing.

The first six hours were black, cold, steep, and unyielding, with the day feeling like it was never going to end. About that time, I asked Vern what the hell he had gotten us into. It was cold, with my feet, fingers, and anything that was exposed on my face feeling numb. In addition, the shale mixed with the rocks made it difficult to find proper footing. The incline never relented, which was draining because we couldn't stand long enough to catch our breath. When friends later asked about the day of the summit and how hard it was to breathe, I described it as if we were running wind sprints for seven hours straight.

All smiles in front of the signpost at Uhuru Peak

Vern and Justin rehydrating at Uhuru

After six and one-half hours of climbing, we could see a pink hue behind a mountain range. It was the sun coming up, which was a welcome sight. The views suddenly became more incredible, and the air began to warm. It was just another memory in a long series of unbelievable experiences.

At this point, Ryan made it just a little bit more enjoyable. He was holding his hands out in front of him, much as a surgeon would after washing his hands before heading into surgery, and he shouted that he couldn't feel his fingers. Maybe if he'd only said it once, it might not have been so memorable; however, after a half dozen times it became funny. At that moment, I asked Emmanuel how much farther. He told me to look over my shoulder. On top of that peak was Uhuru. Once again, I asked how far. He said, "Only forty-five minutes." I began walking faster, when Emmanuel said, *"Pole, pole."*

By then, the climbers who 'd left before us at midnight were starting to descend. I don't know if they could see the exhaustion in our faces, but many of them offered encouragement, saying, "Not much farther."

Even though our pace remained nearly the same, the last half hour seemed to go by quickly, and soon we were at the top, where we hugged one another, laughed, and gave high fives. We then posed for the classic Uhuru sign picture and started heading down the mountain and back to camp. Vern headed down with Sunday, Jill and Ryan were with Philemon, and Julie and I were with Emmanuel.

When we saw the group back down at camp, they talked about how they shale-skied down the mountain and how much fun it was to try. Julie's knee was still hurting, so we took our time getting down the mountain without shale-skiing.

The entire summit climb was a blur. Now it was all about heading down the mountain, which I had not spent much time thinking about, having been so consumed with the thought of summiting. I never thought about going down and what it would entail.

When we reached Mweka Camp, we signed out for the last time. The camp sits dead center of the rainforest, which, in itself, was an incredible experience. Hours ago, we were on top of Uhuru Peak, and now we were in the rainforest. The foliage was thick and damp, yet it still looked extremely comfortable. We anxiously headed to the mess tent for a little celebration and, as always, good conversation.

JILL

After what seemed like ten minutes of shut-eye, my alarm went off. This was by far the coldest I had been. It was hard getting my body outside what little warmth my sleeping bag provided. I hoped that in my dreamlike state, I would also remember to dress appropriately. This was it, the day that would determine success or failure. The excitement and nervousness that ran through my body felt like a constant stream of electricity. My heart was racing. At this moment, all I wanted was for everyone to see the view from the top. I just couldn't imagine getting all this way and not being able to share it with the people who got me this far.

The full moon and the stars cast light on the glaciers on top of Kibo and the peaks that surrounded us. The trail was narrow and covered in loose rock. Darkness surrounded us, as the lights from our headlamps guided our feet at a very slow pace (*pole, pole*). Even walking at a snail's pace, with so much gear on, I started to get hot. I asked Emanuel if I

Ryan and Julie celebrating at Uhuru

could take a layer off before I started to sweat. He assured me that this would quickly pass, and, unfortunately, he was right.

Almost immediately, I began to feel terrible. From one agonizing step to the next, I wondered if I needed to vomit. I could not imagine having to do this in front of a crowd, but I didn't see another alternative at this point. The higher we climbed, the worse I felt. Guides were testing climbers with simple questions and by shining flashlights in their eyes to check their responses. Climbers were dazed and sick all around us, as evidenced by the multiple piles of vomit on the ground. My body knew what it needed to do, and it had to be drastic. I was going to have to fully undress and "make it happen."

I told Philemon that I was feeling sick and needed to stop. He assured me that once he found a "good place" with enough room to step to

Jill and Ryan sharing a celebratory moment at Uhuru

Our guide Emmanuel celebrating our group's achievement

the side, I could take some time to make myself feel better. Once an acceptable spot was found, I walked to a space near a large rock. By that time, I was cold, sick, and scared. As my frozen fingers fumbled to take off my two layers of gloves and four layers of pants, plus underwear, I assumed the position. Ryan, who was concerned about my well-being, turned his headlamp directly at me, casting a perfect spotlight that both blinded me and highlighted one of the most uncomfortable moments of my life. I yelled, "Get that spotlight out of my face!!!" Once he complied with my request, I was able to take care of business and was well enough to return to the hike.

But with each step, it was getting harder to breathe, and at that moment I regretted every cigarette I had smoked in my younger years. The coughing fits slowed my pace, but soon I was able to see the sun starting to make its way to the horizon. Earlier, we'd been told that we would be hitting Stella Point at sunrise. By this time, I could barely lift my legs, feel my body, or breathe. Just when I couldn't stand to walk any farther, I could see a plateau. *It must be Stella Point*, I thought. Once there, we were able to settle in for a few minutes and take in the accomplishment we had achieved.

It was nothing short of spectacular. The sun was beginning to rise, and shades of orange and blue filled the morning sky, while wispy, light clouds floated along the horizon. We all sat down to rest and regroup. This was the moment that my emotions started to get the best of me. I was now confident we were going to make it to the top. After all, we "only" had forty-five more grueling minutes to go. By now, my eyes had started to tear up with joy and excitement. I couldn't believe we were actually going to make it. Each of the guides ran us through some simple tests to make sure our brains were functioning and that we were able to follow instructions and perform simple tasks. When Emanuel came over to check me out, he noticed I was crying. His face became very serious, and I had to reassure him that my tears were tears of happiness and accomplishment, not pain.

The ground that surrounded us was desolate and nearly colorless. This was the first time we were able to see the glaciers up close. They were a grayish-white color, dusted with black dirt arranged in vertical lines, showing the level of snow pack from years past. They stood as tall as a thirty-story building and had grooves that resembled drippy sand castles children often make. It was also the first time we were able to look into the caldera of the volcano, which made my imagination run wild about actually standing at the top of a volcano that at one time had exploded.

As we continued our climb, it became harder to breathe, walk, think, or make any movement that didn't make my head feel like a hatchet was buried in the center of it. Finally, I could see the gathering of people around the sign, taking pictures and celebrating. We had made it! Though Ryan and I have climbed to the tops of many peaks, this was different. We gave each other the biggest hug and kiss. Then the five of us celebrated with heart-filled embraces and words of astonishment, like, "Holy shit, we made it!"

I was so happy for my dad. This was something he had wanted for a lifetime. He had dreamed of standing at this very spot since he was a boy, and here I was to share that moment with him. It was the very reason we were here—to share this goal with him. I was so proud of all of us and felt closer than ever to my family. For that brief fifteen minutes, I didn't notice any aches and pains. I was seriously on top of the world.

We stood in line with all the other climbers for our chance to have our picture taken at the Uhuru sign. Within minutes, we were told to wrap things up and get down the mountain as quickly as possible. We glided down the mountain with huge strides through shale, much like Telemark skiers.

Partway down the mountain, it began to quickly warm up. We made a few short stops to take off clothing and drink water. We were greeted at camp with a fruity orange drink and told we had a few hours to rest before a full day of descending.

After a well-deserved nap, we started the second to the last leg of our trip. By this time, we were already tired from lack of sleep and exhausted from putting our bodies through the most challenging experience of our lives. For motivation, I carried a tiny speaker and played music from a playlist complete with R Kelly, Michael Jackson, Snoop Dogg, and other musical gold from years past. This little bit of music gave me extra pep in my step that I needed at that moment.

Our conversations began to switch gears, and we talked about all the food and the restaurants we missed from home. We also daydreamed about showers and toilets. When we finally made it to camp, all the tents were set up within the trees, which were covered in dangling moss. Once inside our tents, we changed into "fresh" dirty clothes before meeting in the mess hall tent for a popcorn appetizer and Scotch that Vern had in his flask for a toast to our achievement—our first sip of alcohol in days.

Justin celebrating atop Uhuru Peak

RYAN

The final push was an alpine ascent, with us starting in the middle of the night. I was already cold and tired, and, expecting temperatures below zero, I layered up with about every article of clothing I had. Four layers on the bottom included two base layers, alpine pants, and a windbreaker. On top I had two base layers, two middle layer fleeces, and a down puffy jacket covered with a rain/wind shell. About ten layers total. In addition, I wore a neck warmer, a warm hat, alpine gloves, and headphones. You know, typical attire for a midnight stroll.

From the very start of the summit push, the trail was steep. Our elevation was already over 15,000 feet and only going up. We were climbing over 4,000 vertical feet in a three-mile stretch, which is over 1,300 vertical feet per mile in pure darkness. I definitely noticed a difference in breathing.

To compensate, I tried to take deep, slow breaths.

The craziest visual was seeing all the other teams in front of us. They looked like a trail of ants with their headlamps glowing in different colors. It was so dark that we couldn't tell where we were going. So we just followed the lights. At times I would look up and think to myself, *Are you kidding, we're going up there?* It was without a doubt one of my fondest visuals.

After climbing for about three hours, I stopped feeling anything in my toes and fingers—though sometimes there were sharp stinging sensations. After climbing for another hour, I lost all feeling. At this point, I thought something was wrong. Emmanuel checked my fingers and feet for signs of frostbite, making sure that I was okay.

I don't think I've ever experienced a slower pace than those seven grueling hours, about a foot (a single small step) every three to four seconds. While digging up energy for that next step, we could see people turning around and calling it quits and some even having to be carried down with the help of multiple guides. I can't imagine making it that far and having to turn around. The final summit push was tough, and I wondered if there had been an easy way out whether I would have taken it. Probably not, but the thought of turning around did sound nice. But again, turning around was never an option. It was around that time I put in my earphones and cranked the Grateful Dead's "Help on the Way." Hearing the sweet sounds of Jerry Garcia helped me continue, one slow step at a time.

I can't put into words the sense of accomplishment I felt once we finally reached the summit. We'd worked for so many months to make this moment a reality. Now, it was actually happening. It was truly a speechless moment.

We all hugged and cried for several minutes before the guides told us we had to head back down. The pressure at 19,431 feet was too great to stay any longer. Looking back, I can't believe we made it to the roof of Africa. Unbelievable.

Day 7: Our last day! August 11

VERN

We awoke at 6:00 a.m., ready to begin the final descent. Earlier, we had told Philemon that we would skip breakfast to beat the rush to the checkout. Philemon agreed and asked if we had time for the porters to entertain us with some native song and dance. It was a wonderful performance, watching all of the porters and guides singing, dancing, and thanking us for including them on our incredible journey.

The guides addressed each of us to offer congratulations on making it to the summit. In turn, we thanked them for their incredible hospitality and said we wouldn't have made it without their help. As Ryan so eloquently said, "Teaching us that *pole-pole* was more than the speed of our climb—it was a life lesson about appreciating every moment."

It was the perfect ending to the trip.

Of course, we still had to make the five-hour climb to the exit gate, which proved to be a significant challenge for Julie and me, as our knees were severely tested on the slippery trail through the rainforest, over boulders and uneven surfaces.

Stopping for a photo at Stella Point on the way back down

During the first days of our climb, when some of the porters passed us, the odor was noticeable—even from a distance. We decided to rate the body odor on a ten-point scale, with many of them registering a nine or a ten. But after six days on the mountain, we began to notice it less and less, causing us to wonder whether we were acclimating to the odor or if our odor was beginning to match theirs.

Finally, as the trail widened, we saw some young boys selling water and trinkets near the exit gate. The Kilimanjaro beer they sold tasted incredible. We signed out of the park, had one final picture together, and gave some of our extra clothing and equipment to our guides and porters.

Before getting into the Land Rover to leave, I took a moment to say goodbye to the mountain that had haunted me for all those years. She was no longer a dream: she would be an integral part of me from that day forward.

JULIE

I opened my eyes in the tent on our last morning. I knew it would be a very long time before I woke up inside a tent again. Plus, I hadn't had a shower in seven days and was filthy. There was permanent dirt under my short fingernails and a layer of grime and dust that covered my whole body. My hair was matted down under the hat after I'd worn it for almost the entire week. The only part of my body that had touched soap that week were my hands, because that was all I could stand to do in the cold. The only part of me that felt clean was my mouth and that was because Justin and I had brought our electric toothbrushes. All I

Ryan signing out at the exit gate

Vern signing out at the exit gate

could think about was a shower. But we still had one more downward climb to make.

After the customary celebration of songs and dancing put on by the porters and guides, without knowing what to expect, I became pretty emotional. It was such a gift.

After the performance, we got ready to head down to the exit gate. This approximately four-hour climb would take us back down through the rainforest, which would, obviously, make things a bit wet. The going down was slippery at times, but we were able to move at a decent pace. I was so thankful when the narrow path finally opened up to the two-track dirt roadway. We were getting closer! We kept rounding corner after corner, until finally we rounded one final corner and spotted the gate. We had done it! We snapped a picture at the exit sign and got in

Justin signing out at the exit gate

line to sign out. Black-market Kilimanjaro beer was being sold, and we each got an extra-large bottle, which we drank while waiting. As we approached the registry, I felt a bit emotional. I had not been able to sign my own name in one of the books since the first night, as my first priority every night was to get off my feet as quickly as possible. Being able to do this myself gave me much satisfaction.

After that, we were officially done with the climb. Our immediate future involved driving into Moshi to find an ATM, so that we could properly tip our guides and porters. Once that meandering task was completed, we were brought to Mt. Meru Game Lodge, where the staff welcomed us back with smiles and congratulations. I was eager to get to our rooms and into the shower. Tragically, however, there was only enough hot water for each person to take a hot shower for ten seconds, so that luxury was put off for another day. We got cleaned up and headed out to dinner to get our official Mt. Kilimanjaro certificates and to celebrate!

We did it.

JUSTIN

It was our last day on the mountain, and I was a bit sad to be leaving, yet excited to be heading down to the gate. The customary songs and dance by the porters and guides made for an incredible sendoff. This would be the last time we would see most of the porters, and it was a memorable way for them to say goodbye. After they danced and sang, they asked us all to say a few words. After our group talked about the monuments that helped them get to the summit and the memories from the journey, we were off to the gate.

After a few hours, we were at the gate and ready to sign out. We took a few quick photos at the congratulations sign, and we were finished. As we were waiting in line, Vern made eye contact with a porter. The young man came over to ask if he could get us anything. We all instantly responded, in a half joking manner, that we could use a beer. The young man said he'd be right back. Within minutes, he reappeared holding five Kilimanjaro beers. That beer sure tasted great.

After we signed out and before getting back into our jeep, Julie spotted the porter who had helped us with our tent and our sleeping bags. We had already given away much of our gear to Emmanuel and Sunday. As Julie talked with him, I slipped some money to her. We could tell he would be able to put it to good use. Once in the Jeep, we were all sad to be leaving, yet excited to be finished. It had been an incredible challenge. The journey taught me a lot about myself, my wife, my father-in-law, and my sister and brother-in-law.

Thanks, Mt. Kilimanjaro, I will miss you.

JILL

When we woke in the morning, it was such a wonderful thought knowing that this would be the last time I would have to wake up in a sleeping bag. Before leaving, we all stood in a circle and shared what we had taken away from this trip. This was the last leg of our adventure, and we were all ready for it. The ground was soft and muddy, making the descent harder on achy knees. Within a short time, the trail became a road wide enough for a car to pass, and we knew civilization was near. We came to the sign congratulating us on our climb, signifying we had officially made

Informational sign at Mt. Meru Game Lodge,
our home base for most of the trip

it through our entire adventure. What a crazy and successful journey! I couldn't have asked for a better outcome. Asante Sana, Kilimanjaro.

RYAN

I can't think of a more memorable moment than taking that turn from summit push to descent. After working for five straight days, plus a seven-hour push to the top, I was cold and exhausted. The thought of going down put a huge smile on my face, after accomplishing one of my biggest challenges to date. Though emotionally and physically drained, all I could think was, "Thank god that's over with."

The hike down to camp took only two hours. Our guides told us at the summit that we'd have to make it down pretty quickly, since we hadn't been acclimatized to 19,000 feet. The pressure in my head was

Celebrating our climb at the exit gate with some Kilimanjaro beer

so intense, all I could think about was getting back to base camp. The top of the mountain consisted mostly of shale, which made climbing difficult, because as I took one step up, I slid two back. Going down was like sand-skiing. You have your hiking poles for balance, and each stride down probably covered six to eight feet. Although going down might sound fun and easy, it is where you have to be the most careful. The last thing you need at that point is to slip, tumble, and fall thirty or forty feet.

Once back at base camp, we ate some food, then took a long overdue nap. I remember Vern contemplating whether he should call Irene, because it was around 2 a.m. their time. I said something like, "Are you kidding me? You need to call her! You just accomplished your number-one bucket list item."

Chapter 6
NO CAMPFIRES ALLOWED

VERN

As is my nature, I enjoy researching information about the travel adventures Irene and I undertake. I want to know about the people and their language, traditions, social challenges, and opportunities. Although Irene didn't join us on this trip, prior to going, I did extensive research, which saved us a lot of heartache and ultimately contributed to all of us making it to the summit.

Based on my research, I was well aware that the final ascent to Uhuru would be very cold and would have strong winds—things we were well prepared to endure. The one thing that surprised me was the bitter cold that faced us nearly every night on the mountain.

When I added up the estimated climbing times for each day, it appeared there would be significant "down time" following each day's climb. I expected there would be time for a leisurely dinner, followed by telling stories around a campfire or, knowing our family, playing stupid games and reading.

We quickly learned on the first night that campfires were not permitted on Mt. Kilimanjaro. Any visions of bringing a guitar and singing "Kumbaya" were immediately dispelled. One evening we played some Yahtzee, but it only lasted a couple of games, and I have long since forgotten who actually won—though Ryan's victory dance is still etched in my mind.

For me, most evenings consisted of getting situated in our tents (which the porters set up, leaving our large packs inside), a quick wash, and a leisurely dinner, followed by a briefing from one of our guides. After that, it was back to my tent, where I changed into the clothes I would wear the next day. The clothes I'd worn that day were packed around me in the sleeping bag to allow them to dry out. Finally, I would snuggle into my sleeping bag and read from my Kindle for a little while before falling asleep.

When I said snuggle, I meant try to stay warm in any way possible. While I often climbed wearing my base layers, along with a buttoned shirt during the day, as soon as the sun set, the temperatures plummeted. Even at Barafu Camp, the afternoon was sunny and pleasant only hours prior to our summit. However, as the sun went down, bitter cold set in.

In spite of all my planning and purchasing the perfect clothing for the climb, I had decided to rent sleeping bags from the climbing company. It seemed like a good idea, because they would surely be great bags, and it would save space in our limited luggage. They were nice bags, but they didn't match the brutal cold we encountered, and they were "one size fits all," except that Justin's six-foot, four frame barely made it into a bag that was made for someone six feet tall. Should I climb again, I would definitely purchase my own bag.

The Baobab trees are stunning

Understanding our guides was another challenge, which could easily be avoided with better communication on both sides. I knew prior to the climb that guides were not only mandatory, but would be critical in achieving Uhuru. For us to work together, it was important that the guide provide the information required to allow us to be successful. Our guides operated under the premise that we did not want to hear any bad news. This resulted in their avoiding direct responses to our questions. A typical exchange:

"How much longer until we get to camp?"

"Not far," they'd respond when, in reality, it was much farther than we would have guessed. Had we been given information that we were well behind the required pace, we would have shortened our lunch break and increased our pace. Instead, we maintained a pace that delayed

A hippo looks on

our arrival time until after dark. While this might work for others, it was toxic to us.

We resolved this in a meeting with our guides by insisting that they give us straightforward answers, because our group was able to deal with bad news as long as we knew the consequences. It was a critical adjustment in our communication and very helpful as we progressed to the summit, with the guides providing accurate information every half hour describing our progress. When I reflect back, with those two exceptions, there isn't much more I would change.

I am an experienced traveler who very rarely uses a travel agent. However, the extreme challenges of coordinating this trip were significantly streamlined using the services of Eileen, my agent at Frontiers International. She not only knew Tanzania but had summited

Kili the year prior. With her assistance, we scheduled transportation from the airport to our resort, Mt. Meru Game Lodge, which was very helpful since I don't speak Swahili, and our arrival was after dark. The lodge allowed us to store our non-climbing safari gear safely while we were climbing. They also reserved a room for us after our descent.

We decided to wait a day to begin our climb, following our sixteen-hour, seven-time-zone flight, so we could acclimate and enjoy a walking safari in Arusha National Park. The extra day proved very useful in helping us overcome both the jet lag and the effects of high altitude. It also gave us the unique chance to walk with giraffe, zebra, and buffalo.

Similarly, after summiting, we scheduled a three-day reward by traveling to the beautiful resort and coffee plantation at Gibbs Farm, which was the base for our safari through the Ngorongoro Crater. Even the drive to and from the farm was both interesting and educational, as we used the opportunity to meet and learn about the Maasai people who populate the region. Though we were all excited to get back home to loved ones, the extra time was a perfect reward and helpful decompression time, following the intensity of the climb.

My biggest worry was the serious threat posed by altitude. Though our area in Western Michigan is hilly with beautiful ravines and features sand dunes near Lake Michigan, it doesn't offer opportunities to climb at altitude. After a lot of research, I decided to rent an acclimation tent from Hypoxico. It arrived forty-five days prior to our departure and allowed me to gradually increase the simulated altitude, while I worked out on the treadmill with the mask and slept in the tent. Though I believe I would have made the summit without it, I am convinced it made the climb more enjoyable.

As many websites and climbing books explain, your gear is critical, especially boots that are appropriate and well-worn. It is advice I took to heart. I spent a couple of hours at REI, the outfitter, to learn exactly what I would need for each layer of clothing and another hour finding the right boots. I purchased my boots over a year before our departure. That allowed me to log over five hundred miles wearing them, to ensure both the boots and I were ready. Unlike some in our group, I didn't have blisters, nor did I lose any toenails during the climb.

Finally, the best decision I made was to travel with some incredible people who shared my enthusiasm and goal. We each understood— at least, hypothetically—what we were getting into. Each of us trained physically and mentally for the challenge ahead. And, most important, we faced these challenges together as both family and friends.

Using the multitude of resources available to us made our trip an amazing experience and, for me, a life-changing trip of a lifetime.

JULIE

Planning for the trip was a bit crazy. I am not a camper or a generally outdoorsy person and was quite leery about sleeping outside for a week on the mountain. The good news is that at that elevation, there are few bugs and other critters.

My boots were the first item I purchased—a decision I made on my own. For everything else, I relied on Vern's research. He made a trip to the Seattle REI store and got quite an education, which he shared with all of us. Later, he accompanied Justin and me to an REI in Michigan, where we picked out our large backpacks, our Camelback

Moshi

Lookout for spotting elephants and predators—Gibbs Farm

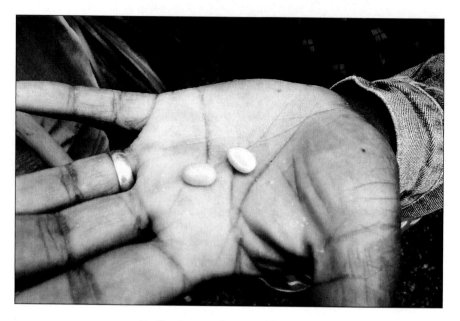

Coffee beans from Gibbs Farm

day packs, socks, balaclavas, sleeping bag liners, pants, shirts, and other items, including base layers. One thing I was amazed by was the amount of gear we had to get. I felt as if all I did in the summer of 2014 was shop, both in stores and on Amazon (our Prime membership was well worth it).

Like most others in our group, I thought there would be some downtime at camp each evening, which is why I brought several books and my iPad. I pulled out my book once and spent way too much time trying to pack the iPad in a way that it would not be damaged.

Here is a list of items that were must-haves for me:

Gallon-sized Ziploc bags were a must for separation and organization of my supplies.

My buff band: This kept dust, sun, wind, and so on, out of my face. It also served as a neck warmer under my balaclava on the summit climb.

A dozen or so microfiber cloths, which we frequently used to clean ourselves.

It was COLD—way colder than we had ever imagined. On most days, if we weren't moving we would freeze. I was alarmed by how cold it was, even on night one. That evening I slept in several layers, along with wearing disposable hand warmers, which I slipped between my socks and gloves while sleeping. On the night before the summit, I slept in every article of clothing I had, which was twenty pieces.

Rent a toilet. The latrines on the mountain were horrific, and sometimes a camp is set up nowhere near one (from our experience, you really don't want to be). At night, close facilities were a luxury.

Female waterbuck with warthog

A Maasai hut

Hand-made Maasai jewelry

Maasai in their traditional clothing

Our water in our Camelbacks froze within two hours into the summit climb, even when we blew back the water out of the tube, as recommended. The only advice I can give is to blow harder and more frequently.

I lost my appetite and had severe digestive distress the day before the summit and could not eat or drink much of anything. The Honey Stinger Organic Energy chews almost literally fueled me up to the top. They were the perfect burst of energy.

Fueling your body is extremely important. My husband and I brought a pound of almonds and something that our kids have dubbed "The Mix." It's a mixture of dried pineapple cubes, chocolate chips, and salted peanuts. We plowed our way through that.

Bring enough cash to tip the guides and porters sufficiently, and then maybe some extra for the guide who carried your gear around and set up your stuff. They earn as little as $6 per week, and any extra cash is always appreciated.

We brought our Sonicare toothbrushes. They were amazing, and held the charge for the entire 15 days of our trip. Being filthy, cold, and dirty was just bearable because my mouth and teeth were squeaky clean and sparkling every morning.

JUSTIN

When mentally prepared, I can generally deal with anything. That said, I wish I had known how cold it was going to be at night.

Cold nights were, by far, the biggest surprise for me on the climb. Of all the articles I had read, none ever mentioned how cold it would be. During our first night at camp, I was amazed at how low the temperature dipped, and by the second night it was unbearable. Before our trip, Julie and I had talked about looking up at the stars without any of the light pollution. But the cold at night made that impossible. There were only fleeting glances while we took brisk walks to our tent. I was well aware of the challenge that the cold would bring on the night of the summit, but even that took me by surprise. I've always been the type of person who hated covering my mouth with clothing when I was outside, but I can promise you that on the night of the summit, the only parts of my face not covered were my eyes.

We were warned about our bladder tubes freezing and about precautions to make sure our bladder lines did not freeze. We were

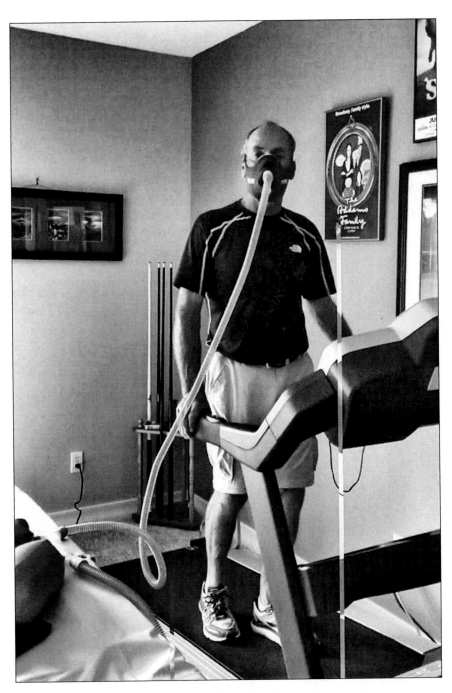

Vern preparing for altitude exercising with mask from Hypoxico unit

School children in Moshi

told multiple times to make sure to blow out the water in the tubes after each sip, but nobody told us that the cold would turn our water bladders into ice blocks an hour into the summit climb. The one missing item I wish I had brought was a thermometer.

Also, I wish I had brought more T-shirts to give to the porters. Those guys do so much with so little and deserve much more than what they are paid. With admiration, I watched as the porters flew by us with bags balanced on top of their heads, while wearing old shoes and shirts.

JILL

Ryan and I did endless hours of research on base layers, comparing different brand names, synthetic materials versus wool and down. This task was more time consuming than we thought it could ever be. The more we shopped around, the more we realized just how much stuff we were going to have to buy to be comfortable on the trip. Going through five different climate changes during the course of the climb meant we basically had to be ready for anything. For myself, natural-based garments worked best. All of my base layers, including my socks, were Merino wool. I also decided on a down jacket because it doesn't hold as much heat when doing extreme activity, while still being warm in the cold. It's only disadvantage is that if it gets wet, drying it out is not possible.

Things getting wet was the number-one concern. We were fortunate not to see any rain. We prepared against rain by keeping our belongings in huge Ziploc bags double-wrapped in garbage bags.

The Maasai

Maasai cattle

We wore gaiters every day, even when it was hot and dusty, which kept moisture away from our feet, along with dust and rocks, which can lead to blisters and cuts.

To help with sleep, I used an over-the-counter sleeping aid, and on more than one occasion I took some Advil PM, which helped with both sleep and sore muscles. I also recommend earplugs. The mountain is a busy place, and tent walls are very thin. There is always someone working, talking, laughing, singing, or washing dishes.

Music is a very important part of my life. I made two different playlists that I kept on my phone. For listening, I brought along a small external speaker and headphones. Our guides also loved music and sang both Tanzanian and American songs.

A waterfall at Arusha National Park

Justin in front of a waterfall

The Maasai

The Maasai

Ryan and I splurged on a few toys, and I think our new camera was the one we used the most, taking over 1,000 pictures. We also bought solar panel chargers that attached to our backpacks, which stored enough energy to charge all our electronics.

Packing for an adventure like this is hard, expensive, and stressful. There are a lot of elements to face, and you need to be prepared. Our guides went over what we'd packed to make sure we had the key essentials we needed. There are some packing lessons on YouTube that I found very helpful. REI and mountaineering stores are another key resource, with people working there more than happy to help.

RYAN

I guess the thing that surprised me most was how cold and tired I was each night. My plan before the trip was to get a good book and enjoy some downtime after each day's climb. That was not the case. After each day, all I wanted to do was eat some food, build up my energy, and get some rest. As we climbed into higher elevations, everything became more difficult, including eating and sleeping.

Of note, after drinking three to four liters of water each day, I woke up every night at least two to three times to relieve myself. Because I was bundled up in multiple layers and there were sub-freezing temperatures outside, going to the bathroom was a hassle. Even though getting out of the tent in sub-freezing temps wasn't ideal, the

We made it!

Zebra at the Ngorongoro Crater

Baby giraffe in Arusha National Park

memory of the luminous stars while it was pitch black was something I will take with me forever.

Another thing I didn't quite get at that time was the sense of accomplishment and pride I'd feel after conquering such a monumental feat. It was worth every punishing moment.

Chapter 7
WOULD YOU DO IT AGAIN?

VERN

It has been over a year since we summited, and each day I still think of the experience. As those around me can attest, I have an incredible passion for talking about the challenges encountered, along with the thrill of reaching the summit. I am fortunate to have a couple of monthly speaking engagements, during which I always insert the picture of us in front of the summit sign on Uhuru. In addition, I wear my Kili Summit Club clothes a few times per week, and I mounted the certificate and the summit picture in the center of my office wall.

I knew the experience would leave a lasting impression, but I never dreamed it would become an obsession. Memories of our climb have become a frequent topic of conversation with my kids and those I meet who have also summited.

A pleasant surprise is that through email and social media, we remain in contact with our guides. My experience is not unique. A friend who summited with her family over five years ago returned to Tanzania recently to visit their guide. In fact, many who summit remain in contact with their guides in some fashion.

By now, I have completely recovered from the climb; however, it took me months to feel completely normal. The most apparent effect was my memory. As we left Mweka Gate, some of the events, including parts of the summit climb, were "foggy" or missing. I noticed it most when it was time to tip the guides and porters. Because I knew credit cards were accepted only in certain areas, I brought a significant amount of cash for tipping during the trip and for making purchases from local vendors. As an experienced traveler, I never put all my cash in one place, instead choosing to hide it in various compartments in my backpacks, luggage, camera bag, and so on. Prior to our climb, I made certain that I would have enough money readily available in my primary day pack to tip the porters and guides the amount recommend by our guide company.

Archway as we approached Kibo

The expansive panoramic views on Kilimanjaro are incredible

It seemed like a perfect plan. However, it became complicated at the outset when we were assigned twenty-one porters, instead of the twelve we were told we would have, and three guides, instead of the two promised. I wasn't concerned, since I had additional money hidden in other compartments.

The plan became murkier during the climb, after we learned that our guide company had recommended a much smaller per day tip for our porters than what was being recommended by organizations like the Kilimanjaro Guides Association.

At Mweka camp, our last night on the mountain, following our celebration and whiskey toast, we tried to work out the math to make certain we would have sufficient funds. I was surprised at how difficult it was for me to make the calculations. I attributed it to having

A view of Lava Tower

Vern on Day 3

Maasai teenager

A trip back from the restroom

summited ten hours earlier and the fact that I was operating on very little sleep.

Luckily, among the five of us, we figured out the amount of money required. Only one small problem, I couldn't remember where I had hidden the extra money. I looked in all the logical places and found nothing. Had it been stolen? It was simply not there, and even with help from the cash the kids brought, we were going to be short.

Upon reaching Mweka Gate, we tipped the porters and two of the guides and informed our lead guide we would have money transferred to a bank in Moshi and could stop to get it on the way to our lodge. Once again, my memory failed me when verifying my identity with questions from my purchases ten years ago, and again with the serious currency conversion challenges.

Julie and Justin

The following day, during a stopover at the Maasai villages while on the four-hour drive to Ngorongoro Crater, I reached for my camera and found one of the elusive hiding places. This happened three more times while accessing various bags, as I discovered my money was exactly where I had hidden it.

This memory loss continued for a couple months following our return home. I would simply lose small amounts of time in total oblivion. Not a daydream, just totally lost time in the middle of a conversation or a work project. Thankfully, I have fully recovered, but it was a strong reminder of the impact of high altitude climbing.

There are two questions commonly asked by friends and family about the climb. The first: What is next on your bucket list?

This is fairly easy to answer. I would love to dive the Great Barrier Reef and explore Australia (there goes that A encyclopedia issue again) and New Zealand. Also high up on my list is climbing Machu Picchu and taking day climbs in the Alps, but this time with Irene. Each of these trips will be separated by some trips to warm destinations in the South Pacific to work on Irene's bucket list.

The other question: Would you do it again? For the first few months after our return, my answer was a quick and definitive, "No."

It's funny, though, how time enhances the memory and diminishes the pain. Julie and Justin's son Bodin has been my buddy since he was an infant. While I enjoy all of our grandchildren, Bodin is the one who likes to hang out with me the most. He was completely infatuated with the climb and the stories we told. Because he was nine at the time we summited, he was much too young to join us on the trip. About three months after our return, he was looking at our summit picture and casually asked how old he would have to be to climb Kili. I told him that I was pretty sure it was sixteen. He then looked me in the eyes and asked, "Papa, would you climb Kili with me when I'm old enough?" How do you say no to that? Today I'm a firm "maybe."

IRENE

I have such a huge sense of pride looking back at the accomplishment of Vern and our kids in climbing Mt. Kilimanjaro. The stories are told over and over, and I never tire of hearing them. All of them stepped out of their comfort zone into an unknown environment and did what they set out to do. How many people can say that?

I know I need to step it up and not let fear get in the way of my decisions. After all, the worst thing that could happen is going to happen eventually. I might as well go out kicking and screaming.

Now I wonder what will Vern's (and my) next adventure be?

JULIE

Climbing Mt. Kilimanjaro was the hardest thing I've ever done. Hands down. And I've had two kids, one without the benefit of an epidural (that was awful, by the way, especially because I was unprepared for it). Climbing Kili is hard enough with a healthy and fit body. Getting injured on the first day and dealing with the associated pain made everything worse (climbing was slower, getting dressed was painful, going to the bathroom was more difficult, sleeping was miserable).

Justin

And it definitely took a toll on my mental state—especially worrying about how my slow pace would affect our group.

From halfway through the first day, virtually every step was excruciating. To illustrate on a pain scale of 1 to 10, at any given moment I was between a 7 and an 8. One wrong step bumped it to a nearly intolerable 9.

Looking back now, I marvel that I got through it. But, through it all, I never thought about turning back. For me, there was only going forward and upward. I learned how the mind can be an incredibly powerful force.

As parents, Justin and I loved the fact that our kids were old enough to understand what we were doing and how hard it really was. Our son Bodin has expressed an interest in climbing a mountain more than once. We're hoping to arrange a one-day climb up Mt. St. Helens next summer with our entire Kili family. But most of all, I love that I got to share the breathtaking and extraordinary experience with my husband and family. It has bonded us in a way that few experiences can.

JUSTIN

A lot of my friends, family, and coworkers ask me if I still think about "the Trip," and I normally respond with "Hell, yes."

Our trip to Mt. Kilimanjaro and reaching Uhuru Peak is not something I'll ever forget. I'm reminded of the climb every time I find myself in a challenging situation. Those so-called difficult moments, which we all have in life, seem to be a little simpler now that I challenged myself and took down the bully of Mt. Kilimanjaro. I explain to people who

Emmanuel, one of our guides

The stunning and rightly famous Shira sunset

Ryan and Jill

Ryan and Jill

are willing to listen that the climb was seriously demanding. The first day was a challenge, just waiting and sitting before we even started our climb. I don't like waiting for anything. I'm the kind of person who believes patience is not a virtue and good things don't come to people who wait. I guess the trip taught me that it is sometimes good to slow down.

That first night sleeping outside in cold weather was not something I expected—not on the first night. That moment helped me in dealing with unexpected issues.

The climbs that should have taken half a day sometimes took the entire day. Those moments helped me realize some projects take longer but are oftentimes worth the wait.

The lack of communication between us and our guides during the day climbs has helped me express myself better.

The night of the summit, when every step was exhausting and each breath of air was a challenge, helped me understand that pain is often required when achieving a goal.

This trip also tested Julie's and my relationship. The fact that I was able to climb with my wife will help us get through any situation that life throws our way, small or large. We have been tested, and I know multitudes of couples who could not have taken this trip and survived each other. In my opinion, we passed with flying colors.

The trip has brought me closer to family on the other side of our country, family that I absolutely love. We will always have an inspiring trip to discuss with one another.

The trip allowed us to demonstrate to our kids that hard work pays off. They witnessed us working out daily to make sure we were in shape to make our final goal to the top of Uhuru Peak. Any time you can show your kids how hard work pays off is good.

The trip allowed me to take a trip with a good friend, my father-in-law, the man who dreamed about a mountain and a climb from when he was a child and made it a reality for all five of us. He is an inspiring person who has reinforced my beliefs that anything can be accomplished with hard work and the correct frame of mind.

JILL

In the months that followed, I found myself talking about my experience daily. As a physical therapy assistant, a huge part of my job is encouraging people and letting them know they are capable of achieving physical goals they set for themselves. Hearing the story about my father climbing Mt. Kilimanjaro with two very old titanium knees is incredibly helpful to people. They are impressed because of his age and because he, too, was in the same situation, where simply bending his knee or walking was painful. I enjoy being able to use my dad as an example of what a person can achieve by following his dreams, and to reinforce the idea that nobody should use age as an excuse, but should live a healthy life, even if you have to struggle with setbacks. His story gives them hope, even if they don't want to climb a mountain. They know that with some determination, they might be able to at least take a walk in a park without pain.

When we first got home, people generally asked two questions about our experience. "Would you do it again?" and "What mountain is next?" Without skipping a beat, I'd say that I had no desire to challenge myself like that again. My next vacation was going to have sandy beaches, sun, showers, and the "oh so difficult task" of deciding on which flavor of blended drink would start my day. However, since time has passed, the struggles, the lack of showers, and the cold weather have become a minuscule part of an exciting journey. Now, I would certainly climb Mt. Kilimanjaro again. Not to relive the experience, but to have a completely new one. What we experienced changed me and brought me closer to the people I love. I will always have the desire to hike and climb mountains, and there are so many beautiful

Ryan with the giraffes we saw on our pre-climb trek
around Arusha National Park

places I would love to explore. But I am positive Mt. Kilimanjaro will be the tallest mountain I will ever climb.

I feel a special connection to Mt. Rainer. Some days you can't even see the 14,000-foot freestanding mountain, due to clouds, but when it is visible, it's impossible not to be awed by its beauty. It is a view that never gets boring or old. Although it is a lower mountain by almost a mile, the glaciers covering Mt. Rainer make it a more difficult and technical climb than Mt. Kilimanjaro. One day I know I will stand at the top.

As often as possible, I have enjoyed traveling and exploring. Our Kilimanjaro trip was one of the most influential trips of my life. It has been over a year since I placed my feet on the top of the tallest freestanding mountain in the world. To be able to say that I could share this accomplishment with my family makes it even more special. To share in a moment that my father dreamed about his whole life makes it even more amazing. Being able to kiss my husband at 19,000 feet was incredible. To share moments of laughter, frustration, accomplishment, fatigue, astonishment, fear, and pure joy with Julie and Justin and coming away closer to them than I have ever been before is priceless. I look back on the trip feeling fortunate to have been able to learn about an amazing culture, while exploring countless miles of the earth that are vastly different from any I have seen before. I feel more alive knowing that I have tested my body with an experience many people might not be able to handle. I am lucky to have taken on such a challenge and managed to come out on top.

RYAN

Even though it's been well over two years since we returned from Mt. Kilimanjaro, it still seems like yesterday, but also a lifetime ago. When asked if the climb is something I still think about, I'd say a definite yes.

I have a couple of pictures mounted in my office as reminders. Mainly, I think about our guides and wonder how they're doing. It is a very pleasant surprise that we are able to remain in contact with our guides through Facebook. I like hearing stories of the new groups going up and down the mountain. Also, I think about the wellbeing and working conditions of the porters. We started a business because of the emotional connection we now have with the region. Kili Summit Club was created to help give back to the Kilimanjaro community. It's pretty cool, and I hope you check it out. Forty percent of all profits go

A porter trying to get reception

back to the porters, by either supplying more modern equipment or taking care of hospital bills, due to injury on the mountain.

I have heard from a number of people about how Mt. Kilimanjaro changed their lives. For me, it's more about the things I've taken away from the trip. *Pole-pole,* for example. That mantra has helped me in my daily life, whether it's working on my relationship with Jill, remembering to slow things down and look at the big picture, or at work on daily tasks. I've learned to try and not rush through things, enjoy my surroundings, and make sure my current course is on track. Would I do something like this again? Absolutely. Just tell me when and where. My next vacation, though, was the complete opposite. It was sipping margaritas in Mexico to My Morning Jacket's "One Big Holiday."

Chapter 8

FOR THOSE CRAZY ENOUGH TO GO

VERN

Although I made many good decisions in my preparation, clearly there are things I would do differently if I were to climb again.

First and most important, I would bring my own sleeping bag, and I would make certain that it would exceed the severe temperatures on the mountain. We were all aware of the extreme temperatures at the summit. However, beginning with the second night it was very cold as soon as the sun set. There are no campfires on the mountain, and the only source of heat is derived from hand and foot warmers brought along and body heat. We trusted our guide company to provide the bags, and they were seriously inadequate for the temperatures we endured.

Living in Western Michigan, we experience very cold temperatures in the winter months. I trained during one of our coldest winters in decades prior to our climb, invested in some quality outdoor gear, and remained very comfortable. What I didn't understand is that the climb to the summit is incredibly slow. While doing my workouts in

This smile says it all

the cold at home, I was able to keep a very steady and comfortable pace, which helped to keep my feet and hands warm, even in the most severe blizzards. Ascending the final summit push, you barely move, with the final three to four hours requiring a stop after each step. My down-filled mittens were a lifesaver, and the foot warmers in my boots kept my feet from getting frostbite.

We have mentioned the value we placed on Tent #1 in previous chapters, and I would reinforce that conviction again. From the very first day, the guides repeatedly monitor climbers' liquid intake and constantly reinforce the idea that drinking a minimum of three liters of water every day during the climb is critical to avoiding altitude sickness and reach Uhuru. In addition to this constant hydration, each meal featured tea coupled with either porridge or soup. While the body absorbs much of this constant intake of liquids, a lot of it is eliminated. For me, it was eliminated primarily during the night. Two to three times each night, I would grudgingly leave the warmth of my sleeping bag, put on my boots, and trudge over to Tent #1 to relieve myself. Bringing a container to void into while still in my sleeping bag would be a serious priority for me on the next climb.

While I believe that I would have made it to the summit without it, I am convinced that renting the altitude acclimation tent from Hypoxico allowed me to ascend to Uhuru without any of the signs of altitude sickness. Every sensation that I experienced regarding altitude, with the exception of the hallucinations on the summit climb, I had overcome while using the tent and the face mask. As soon as I began to feel lightheaded, I knew that I could counter this with deep sustained breaths, and the headache would pass. I was able to reach my ultimate goal without any serious concerns that altitude sickness would threaten my success.

Be aware that the number of porters and guides is very fungible. We used a very reputable travel agency, which recommended a guide company that it frequently recommended to high-end travelers. We were informed that we would have twelve porters and two guides for our climb. At the Machame Gate, we were informed that we were assigned three guides, twenty porters, and a cook. This dramatically changed the amount of cash required for the tips at the end of the climb. The nine additional porters, plus the additional guide, increased our tip total to $880, and they don't accept credit cards! Ouch.

Our guides were willing to stop at a bank so we could withdraw some cash with our debit card. However, the ATM dispenses only approximately $60 US per transaction. Fortunately, AMEX was able to wire me about $1,500 US to a local bank. Of course, the bank dispensed my money in Tanzanian shillings. As I write this, there are slightly more than 2,000 Tz shillings per 1 US dollar. Strangely, the largest denomination the bank dispensed was 30,000 Tz shilling notes. That's right, it dispensed $1,500 in the equivalent of 15 dollar bills. I summoned all four kids and asked them to stuff handfuls of bills into their pockets as we exited the bank, passing the Uzi-carrying armed guards and quickly entering our transport vehicle as our driver sped off. Once cleared of the busy city streets, Jill proudly proclaimed, "I'm holding a million dollars!"

Tipping is a really big deal to both the guides and the porters. Too many guide companies claim to pay fair wages, only to keep much of the money for profit. Please check with the Kilimanjaro

On the top of Barranco Wall

I'm holding a million dollars!

The birds of Kilimanjaro

Guides Association, *www.kilimanjaroguidesassociation.org,* and the Kilimanjaro Porters Assistance Project, *www.kiliporters.org,* to make certain that your guide company meets the minimum standards of these two nonprofit organizations regarding the compensation and treatment of porters.

JULIE

Summing up in one sentence: climbing Mt. Kilimanjaro caused me the most elation and the most misery that I've ever experienced in my life.

As with many painful and difficult experiences, my recollection has fuzzed over a bit on the more trying portions of the climb. This is evidenced by my response as to whether I'd do it again. In

Julie and a happy porter

Shira Camp

A porter carrying a typical load

the immediate months after the climb, it was a quick and emphatic, "NO!" But now I look back at the highlights with the same amount of wonder, pride, and thrill, and even harder times are remembered with more fondness. I've actually said on more than one occasion that I'd consider climbing it again—especially since our ten-year-old son has expressed an interest in climbing it himself. For the record, our eight-year-old daughter is a solid "maybe."

Preparing for this trip was like no other, especially for this novice mountain climber. Not only did we need to first research, purchase, and pack enough "core" gear (backpacks, pants, shirts, pillow, etc.), we "needed" dozens of other items that provided comfort or convenience, including microfiber towels, lip balm, snacks, chafing cream (never ended up using that), books, and an iPad (dumbest item I brought). And while our porters carried our large backpacks up and down the mountain and set them in our tents each evening, we still needed to nearly unpack all items each evening and then repack them the next morning—all the while absolutely freezing, occasionally nauseous, and, in my case, with some serious knee pain. It made maneuvering around the tent, rolling up the sleeping bag, and packing immeasurably painful.

If you are crazy enough to climb Mt. Kilimanjaro, here are some things to consider. Because it was both my first mountain and first camping experience, in retrospect, there were half a dozen things I could have done (or brought) to make the experience more comfortable—none of which occurred to me beforehand.

We went in August, which is one of the more favorable months to attempt to summit. Though we brought rain pants (which served us well on summit day), we never encountered any real precipitation.

Looking back and reading through other people's experiences made me realize how very lucky we were. Miserable weather can add layers of complications by way of gear not drying out right, feet becoming wrinkled and soggy, and paths becoming slippery. Though we knew we had the weather on our side, due to the month we chose, it was wise to prepare for all weather situations.

Prepare to get dirty and stinky. Really stinky. Because the climb starts out in a rainforest near the equator, we started out the climb in some light layers, which were quickly discarded. I unzipped my convertible pants at the knees about an hour into the climb because I got so warm. By the time we got to the first camp, we were all sweaty. There were no showers available, of course, but each morning Kennedy/Duncan set out a small bowl of warm water, which we were to use for a sponge bath of sorts. This was nice on the first day, but each subsequent morning the water cooled off by the time we were ready to use it, because camp in the morning was just so damn cold. This made stripping down to "bathe" less appealing each day. I think by Day 3 I gave up on the "wash-wash" and used wipes, which got pretty bad. Be sure to bring enough baby wipes and microfiber towels.

I had done very little reading about what people experienced on Mt. Kilimanjaro (intentionally), so I didn't have any concrete expectations about the journey. I knew it would be cold, but I didn't realize how cold it would get—our water froze in our Camelbacks on the summit climb. We got back from the day's climb, cleaned up for dinner, and then it was back into several layers of clothing inside our tents. I knew we would be hiking for many hours every day, but I didn't realize how challenging those hikes would be, going up and over enormous boulders, down endless valleys, and then right back up the other side,

Justin talking to a Maasai chief

Jill, the "12th man"

all the while at a snail's pace because of my injury. I knew the summit climb would be hard but didn't realize the exhaustion would pile up from the previous days (plus, unexpected gastrointestinal distress and a bum knee), which would make the summit push so challenging. However, I wouldn't change anything about my mental preparation. My advice is to hope for the best, but be prepared for any unknown that could get tossed your way. I was completely unprepared for my knee to give out on Day 1; thankfully, Jill brought Kinesio tape, and Vern brought a knee wrap that saved me.

The best advice I could give anyone crazy enough to consider climbing Mt. Kilimanjaro is: If someone invites you to go, say, "YES." Just go. One could find a million excuses not to go (I tried to come up with a few of my own when making the decision), but I know that I would have regretted it every day for the rest of my life if I (we) had chosen to miss out on this adventure.

Our shared experience not only brought my family and me closer to one another, but as a result of the trip, we started a very unique business, Kili Summit Club, that will forever unite us with Mt. Kilimanjaro and the people there. Through KSC, Kili is on our minds every single day. I love how I'll be wearing my Bragging Gear, and people will come up to me and share their climbing experiences. Just a week ago, I met someone who had summited Kili twice. It's amazing how many people have a connection to Mt. Kilimanjaro.

Vern, I am forever grateful for the awe-inspiring invitation that you so graciously extended to Justin and me. I had no idea what we were getting into and am so thankful we said yes. I love you. Jill and Ryan, I feel so fortunate for the opportunity to have climbed this mountain

Ryan, the "12th man"

with you two. I love that this experience brought us closer, even from all the way across the country. Traveling with you guys was so much fun, and I couldn't imagine embarking on the trip without you. Mom, I never could have left our kiddos on one continent while departing for another without you. Knowing that they were safe, entertained, and showered with love while in your care gave me more peace of mind that I can ever express. Thank you for being there for our family—without hesitation—over and over again. I love you. Justin, hon, I still can't believe we did this together. I love how you helped me through the most difficult experience of my life so perfectly—and only the way you can (and yes, I'm officially declaring that climbing Mt. Kilimanjaro is infinitely harder than childbirth). I love the example we've set for the kids, and I so look forward to our next adventure. I love you!

Certificates confirming we made it to the top

JUSTIN

If I were to climb Mt. Kilimanjaro again, I would know what to expect in terms of the weather. In addition, I would make sure to take the trip with a group of people that I respect and that I want to share a lifetime of memories with. Obviously, there was an incredible amount of effort that went into preparing for our trip. Having the correct clothing, the training, and all other preparation is a must. But the two most important factors are being prepared to be uncomfortable and having people you respect—and that you want to be with while being uncomfortable.

The lack of comfort started on Day 1, as we began the trip in a rainforest and the first night sleeping on a slanted mountain in the cold. The discomfort for me did not end until four months later, when my toenail finally fell off.

I can't imagine being on the side of Mt. Kilimanjaro, trying to get to the summit with people who were not one hundred percent committed to the same goal. This I say because climbing that bully with my family meant putting every selfish agenda to the side to make sure we all got to the top. It is impossible to put into words how much pride it gave me.

I would oftentimes repeat the phrase, "Pain is temporary, pride lasts forever," which was what my favorite guide, Emmanuel, told us on the night we began our summit. It was a phrase I had not heard before taking our incredible journey, but now it lives with me daily.

JILL

Climbing a massive mountain is not for most people. Let's face it. The trip is very expensive, and it requires a certain amount of physical strength and endurance. Once you're there, it is dirty, sweaty, exhausting, dangerous, cold, painful, and uncomfortable. This kind of trip is not even a possibility for most people. However, even after every negative adjective I described, I feel like we are the lucky ones for being able to make Mt. Kilimanjaro a part of our life's story. There are very few things in life more rewarding than having a goal and being able to achieve it. Many people set goals for their career, school, and family. Setting a physical goal is also rewarding because it challenges your body, mind, heart, and soul. If you are one of the fortunate ones to be able to make this experience part of your life, DO IT!

Our incredible view once we scaled the Barranco Wall

One of the most memorable and lasting parts of this epic adventure was being able to share it with my family and my husband. I would not have changed those who surrounded me for anything in the world.

The trek to Uhuru has been a spiritual journey for people for thousands of years. I can only assume that if this trek could bring my family as close as it did, it can do the same for others.

The wonderful thing about Mother Nature is that the world is ever changing. Nobody else will ever have the same experience we had. The cloud cover is ever changing, the vegetation will be older, and the weather will be different. The glaciers are forever changing.

Save up, train, and make this adventure happen so you can have your own story to tell.

RYAN

If you're reading this and considering the trip, make it happen. You'll be glad you did. I pushed myself to whole new levels, had an incredible bonding experience with my family, and grew closer to my wife. A win-win all around. Thank you, Vern, for making this a reality.

VERN

In closing, I strongly recommend climbing with a close friend or relative. At one point, it was looking like I would be climbing on my own, which I would have done, if it came to that. Luckily, two of my daughters and their husbands joined me on this incredible adventure. In addition, I was able to speak to Irene every night via cell phone and share the memories and challenges of the day. Having them there with me was an incredible experience, but being able to relive the climb and the trip is, as they say, priceless. It is a bond that we will share for the rest of our lives.